A COMPLETE GUIDE TO INTERNSHIPS

DR. ANUJA PANDEY

Copyright © Dr. Anuja Pandey
All Rights Reserved.

This book has been self-published with all reasonable efforts taken to make the material error-free by the author. No part of this book shall be used, reproduced in any manner whatsoever without written permission from the author, except in the case of brief quotations embodied in critical articles and reviews.

The Author of this book is solely responsible and liable for its content including but not limited to the views, representations, descriptions, statements, information, opinions and references ["Content"]. The Content of this book shall not constitute or be construed or deemed to reflect the opinion or expression of the Publisher or Editor. Neither the Publisher nor Editor endorse or approve the Content of this book or guarantee the reliability, accuracy or completeness of the Content published herein and do not make any representations or warranties of any kind, express or implied, including but not limited to the implied warranties of merchantability, fitness for a particular purpose. The Publisher and Editor shall not be liable whatsoever for any errors, omissions, whether such errors or omissions result from negligence, accident, or any other cause or claims for loss or damages of any kind, including without limitation, indirect or consequential loss or damage arising out of use, inability to use, or about the reliability, accuracy or sufficiency of the information contained in this book.

Made with ♥ on the Notion Press Platform
www.notionpress.com

Contents

"Intellectual growth should commence at birth and cease only at death." — Albert Einstein

In today's competitive job market, securing a fulfilling and successful career often starts well before graduation. Internships serve as a crucial stepping stone, acting as a "runway to success" for aspiring professionals. They offer an array of opportunities and experiences that prepare individuals for future careers. Internship is a key to launching a successful professional journey.

Embarking on an internship can be a transformative experience, allowing individuals to gain valuable skills, make connections, and explore their passions. Internships are incredibly valuable experiences for students and young professionals.

Introduction to Internships

Internships are a valuable opportunity to gain practical experience, build professional skills, and explore career paths. Whether you're a student or a recent graduate, taking advantage of internship opportunities can be a significant step toward your career goals. Absolutely, an internship can be seen as a door to success, offering a range of opportunities that can significantly impact your professional and personal development. Internships are a strategic way to advance your career by providing valuable experience, skills, and connections. By approaching internships with a proactive and goal-oriented mindset, you can effectively use them as a springboard to achieve your career aspirations.

An internship is a period of work experience offered by an organization for a limited period of time. Internships are typically aimed at students or recent graduates to provide them with practical experience in their field of study or career interest. They can vary widely in terms of duration, scope, and whether they are paid or unpaid. The primary purpose of internships is to bridge the gap between academic learning and practical application. Here's a breakdown of the main purposes:

1. Professional Experience

- **Hands-On Learning:** Internships offer real-world experience that allows individuals to apply theoretical knowledge gained through academic studies in a practical setting. In internships, a methodical approach effectively bridges theoretical knowledge with practical experience, greatly enhancing skill acquisition and professional development. Preparing for a hands-on internship requires thorough research and planning. This starts with a clear understanding of the role itself. Researching the specific tasks and responsibilities associated with the internship position is crucial. This helps in setting realistic expectations and preparing adequately for the responsibilities at hand. Equally important is seeking regular clarification and feedback to deepen one's understanding of the role. This ongoing dialogue helps in adjusting and refining one's approach to the tasks and challenges encountered. Viewing problems as opportunities for learning and adapting strategies accordingly is key to growth. Regular reflection on what has worked well and what hasn't been necessary for continuous improvement and effective problem-solving. Collaborating with colleagues and mentors is also a significant aspect of the internship experience. Engaging with others allows for gaining diverse perspectives, which can lead to improved outcomes and richer learning experiences. It's important to communicate ideas clearly and provide constructive feedback to others, fostering a collaborative and supportive work environment. Setting personal learning objectives and career goals provides direction and focus throughout the internship. This involves defining what one hopes to achieve and the skills one aims to develop. By aligning the internship experience with these goals, one can maximize the benefits and ensure that the experience contributes meaningfully to both immediate and long-term career aspirations.

- **Skill Development:** Interns develop and enhance specific skills related to their field, such as technical abilities, project management, and industry-specific practices. Internships serve as a crucial bridge between academic learning and real-world application, offering invaluable opportunities for skill development. The process of skill enhancement during an internship is multifaceted and begins with a proactive approach to understanding and integrating into the work environment. Interns are typically exposed to a range of tasks and responsibilities that are directly relevant to their field of study or career aspirations. This exposure provides a practical context in which theoretical knowledge can be applied, tested, and refined. Initially, understanding the scope and nature of the internship role is fundamental. Interns must familiarize themselves with the specific tasks they will be handling and the expectations of their role within the organization. This involves not only learning the technical aspects of the job but also grasping the broader goals and objectives of the team or department. Such an understanding helps interns align their efforts with the organization's needs, thereby contributing more effectively and gaining a clearer picture of how their work fits into the larger picture. Effective communication is a critical skill that is developed and honed during an internship. Interns must regularly seek clarification on tasks and responsibilities to ensure they meet expectations. This ongoing dialogue with supervisors and colleagues helps in addressing any uncertainties and adapting to new challenges. Interns also benefit from providing and receiving constructive feedback, which fosters a culture of continuous improvement and personal growth. By actively engaging in these interactions, interns can refine their ability to articulate ideas clearly and respond to feedback in a constructive manner. Another important aspect of skill development during an internship is the ability to handle problems and challenges creatively. Interns often encounter situations that require innovative thinking and problem-solving skills. Viewing these challenges as learning opportunities rather than obstacles encourages a proactive and resilient mindset. Adapting strategies based on feedback and reflection is essential for overcoming difficulties and achieving better results. Interns who regularly reflect on their experiences and assess what worked well or didn't can develop more effective approaches to future tasks. Collaboration plays a significant role in skill development during internships. Working closely with colleagues and mentors provides interns with diverse perspectives and insights that enrich their learning experience. This collaborative environment helps interns build strong professional relationships and learn from the expertise of others. By engaging in team projects and participating in discussions, interns can enhance their teamwork and interpersonal skills, which are crucial for success in any professional setting. Setting personal goals is another critical element in maximizing the benefits of an internship. Interns should define clear learning objectives and career aspirations to guide their efforts throughout the internship. These goals help in maintaining focus and motivation, ensuring that the experience aligns with their long-term career plans. By regularly evaluating progress towards these goals, interns can make adjustments as needed and ensure they are developing the skills and competencies that are most relevant to their career aspirations. In summary, internships provide a rich environment for skill development through practical experience, effective communication, problem-solving, collaboration, and goal-setting. By actively engaging in these areas, interns can enhance their professional capabilities and prepare themselves for future career challenges. The skills acquired during an internship are not only valuable for immediate tasks but also lay a strong foundation for long-term professional growth and success.

1.2. Career Exploration

- **Industry Insight:** Internships provide exposure to the day-to-day operations of a profession, helping individuals understand the industry better. Internships offer a unique vantage point for gaining industry insight that goes far beyond what is taught in a classroom. They immerse individuals in the daily operations and culture of a specific field, providing a comprehensive understanding of industry practices and trends. This first-hand experience is invaluable for those looking to enter a particular profession or advance their career within it. From the outset, internships provide a direct connection to the real-world application of industry knowledge. Interns are often involved in tasks and projects that reflect current industry standards and practices. This exposure allows them to see how theoretical concepts are applied in practical scenarios, bridging the gap between academic learning and industry realities. Observing and participating in these processes helps interns grasp the nuances of their chosen field, including the workflows, technologies, and methodologies that are commonly used. Additionally, internships offer an opportunity to understand industry-specific challenges and opportunities. Interns can gain insights into the obstacles that professionals face on a daily basis, as well as the strategies and solutions employed to overcome these challenges. This exposure helps interns develop a more realistic and informed perspective on what working in the industry entails. It also enables them to appreciate the dynamic nature of the field, including how it evolves in response to technological advancements, market demands, and other external factors. Networking is another critical aspect of gaining industry insight through internships. Interns have the chance to build relationships with industry professionals, including mentors, colleagues, and supervisors. These connections can provide valuable guidance, advice, and insider knowledge about the industry. Engaging with experienced professionals allows interns to learn from their experiences, gain career advice, and understand industry expectations and norms. Networking also opens doors for future opportunities, such as job placements, recommendations, and collaborations. Furthermore, internships offer a window into the organizational culture of the industry. Understanding the culture of a company or organization is crucial for career development, as it affects everything from work practices to interpersonal relationships. Interns can observe how teams interact, how decisions are made, and how the organization navigates industry trends and challenges. This cultural insight helps interns determine whether they align with the values and practices of the industry and prepares them for successful integration into similar environments. Internships also provide a platform for interns to explore different roles and career paths within the industry. By working in various capacities and participating in diverse projects, interns can identify their interests and strengths. This exploration helps them make more informed decisions about their career direction and specialization. It also allows them to assess which aspects of the industry resonate with them and where they might want to focus their future efforts. In addition to technical and practical insights, internships offer a broader perspective on industry trends and future directions. Interns are often exposed to strategic discussions and planning sessions that reveal how organizations anticipate and adapt to changes in the industry. This exposure helps interns understand emerging trends, technological advancements, and shifts in market dynamics. Being aware of these factors equips them with the knowledge to anticipate future developments and adapt their career strategies accordingly. Internships provide a rich source of industry insight by offering practical experience, exposure to industry challenges and opportunities, networking opportunities, cultural understanding, and a broader perspective on industry trends. This comprehensive view not only enhances interns' immediate understanding of their field but also prepares them for future career success by aligning their skills and expectations with industry realities. The knowledge and connections gained during an internship are invaluable assets that contribute to long-term professional growth and career advancement.

- **Role Familiarity:** They help interns learn about different roles within the industry and determine which career path might be the best fit for them. Gaining role familiarity during an internship is a critical component of professional development. It encompasses understanding the specific tasks, responsibilities, and expectations associated with a given position within an organization. This understanding is essential for interns to effectively contribute to their teams and to maximize their learning experience. From the beginning, establishing a clear understanding of the role is crucial. Interns need to become acquainted with the scope of their responsibilities and the nature of the work they will be involved in. This often involves reviewing job descriptions, discussing expectations with supervisors, and gaining insights from colleagues who have experience in similar roles. By doing so, interns can align their efforts with the organization's objectives and ensure that they are prepared to meet the demands of their position. Immersing oneself in the daily tasks associated with the role helps interns to become familiar with the practical aspects of their job. This may include learning specific procedures, mastering relevant software or tools, and understanding the workflow of the team or department. Hands-on experience with these tasks allows interns to apply theoretical knowledge in real-world contexts, thereby reinforcing their learning and improving their competency in performing job-related functions. An important aspect of role familiarity involves understanding how one's role fits into the larger organizational structure. Interns should strive to grasp how their responsibilities contribute to the overall goals of the organization. This perspective helps interns appreciate the significance of their work and motivates them to perform their duties with a sense of purpose and accountability. It also fosters an understanding of how different roles within the organization interact and collaborate to achieve common objectives. Regular communication with supervisors and colleagues is essential for gaining and maintaining role familiarity. Interns should actively seek feedback and clarification on their tasks and responsibilities. This ongoing dialogue helps in addressing any uncertainties and adjusting performance to better meet expectations. Additionally, asking questions and seeking advice from more experienced professionals provides valuable insights into the nuances of the role and helps interns refine their approach to their work. As interns become more familiar with their roles, they should also reflect on their experiences to identify areas for improvement. Regular self-assessment and reflection on what has been successful and what challenges have arisen can guide interns in refining their skills and adapting their strategies. This reflective practice allows interns to continuously enhance their performance and better understand the intricacies of their role. Moreover, engaging in additional projects or tasks beyond the core responsibilities can further deepen role familiarity. Volunteering for extra assignments or participating in cross-functional projects provides interns with a broader view of the organization and helps them develop a more comprehensive understanding of their role. This proactive approach not only demonstrates initiative but also enriches the internship experience by exposing interns to a wider range of activities and responsibilities. Building relationships with mentors and colleagues also contributes to a better understanding of the role. These relationships offer support and guidance, providing interns with insights into best practices and strategies for success. Mentors can share their experiences and offer advice on navigating challenges, while colleagues can provide practical tips and support for daily tasks. Role familiarity during an internship is achieved through a combination of understanding job responsibilities, gaining practical experience, and aligning one's role with organizational goals. Effective communication, ongoing reflection, and proactive engagement in additional tasks all contribute to a deeper understanding of the position. By immersing themselves in the role and seeking feedback and guidance, interns can develop a robust understanding of their job, which enhances their ability to contribute effectively and prepares them for future career opportunities.

1.3. Networking Opportunities

- **Professional Connections:** Internships allow individuals to build relationships with professionals, mentors, and peers in their field. Professional connections made during an internship are among the most valuable aspects of the experience. These connections encompass relationships with colleagues, supervisors, mentors, and industry professionals, and they play a crucial role in shaping an intern's career. Building and nurturing these connections not only enhance the internship experience but also lay a foundation for future professional growth and opportunities. One of the primary benefits of developing professional connections during an internship is the access to mentorship. Interns often have the opportunity to work closely with experienced professionals who can provide guidance, support, and feedback. Mentors serve as valuable resources, offering insights into industry practices, career advice, and personal development strategies. They can help interns navigate the complexities of their roles, offer constructive criticism, and provide encouragement, all of which contribute to the intern's growth and confidence in their abilities. Networking within an organization also facilitates a deeper understanding of its culture and dynamics. Building relationships with colleagues and supervisors allows interns to observe and integrate into the organizational environment more effectively. These interactions help interns grasp the unwritten norms and expectations of the workplace, which can significantly impact their success and integration into the team. By understanding and adapting to the organizational culture, interns can align their work with the values and goals of the organization, thereby enhancing their contributions and potential for future opportunities. Engaging with colleagues on various projects and tasks fosters collaboration and teamwork skills. Working alongside professionals in different roles provides interns with a broader perspective on how various functions within the organization interact and contribute to overall objectives. These collaborations help interns build a network of contacts within the organization, each of whom can offer different insights and expertise. The ability to work effectively in a team setting and to manage interpersonal relationships is a crucial skill that can be developed through these interactions. Beyond the immediate workplace, internships often provide opportunities to connect with professionals in the broader industry. Many organizations host networking events, conferences, or workshops that interns can attend. These events offer a platform to meet industry leaders, peers from other organizations, and professionals with similar interests. Establishing connections at these events can be instrumental in learning about industry trends, exploring career opportunities, and gaining a broader perspective on the field. These external connections can also serve as valuable contacts for future job searches or career advice. Maintaining and leveraging these professional connections after the internship is crucial for long-term career development. Keeping in touch with mentors, colleagues, and industry contacts can provide ongoing support and guidance throughout one's career. Regular communication, whether through emails, LinkedIn updates, or occasional meetings, helps to sustain these relationships and keep one's professional network active. By staying connected, interns can benefit from continued advice, potential job referrals, and updates on industry developments. In addition to practical benefits, professional connections formed during an internship can offer personal growth opportunities. Building relationships with a diverse group of professionals allows interns to gain new perspectives, learn from different experiences, and develop a more well-rounded view of their chosen field. These interactions can inspire new ideas, motivate personal development, and foster a sense of belonging within the industry. Furthermore, professional connections often lead to opportunities for career advancement. Interns who cultivate strong relationships and demonstrate their value through their work are more likely to be considered for future job openings within the organization or receive recommendations for positions elsewhere. Positive connections with industry professionals can also lead to invitations for further networking opportunities, involvement in industry-specific projects, or collaborations that enhance one's career profile. Professional connections made during an internship are invaluable for both immediate and long-term career development. These relationships offer mentorship, insights into organizational culture, collaborative experiences, and broader industry exposure. Maintaining and leveraging these connections can provide ongoing support, career opportunities, and personal growth. By actively building and nurturing professional relationships, interns can enhance their internship experience and set a solid foundation for future career success.

- **Future Opportunities:** Networking can lead to future job prospects, mentorship, and professional collaborations. The importance of building professional connections during an internship cannot be overstated, particularly when considering how these relationships influence future opportunities. An internship is not just a period of gaining hands-on experience and developing skills; it is also a crucial time for establishing a network of contacts that can significantly impact one's career way. The connections made during an internship can open doors to numerous opportunities, both immediately and in the long term, making the process of networking a key component of career development. One of the most immediate benefits of forging strong professional connections during an internship is the potential for job offers. Interns who build positive relationships with their colleagues, supervisors, and other professionals are often considered for full-time positions within the organization. When an organization is familiar with an intern's work ethic, skills, and cultural fit, they are more likely to extend a job offer upon the completion of the internship. This is particularly advantageous as it can streamline the job search process and reduce the uncertainty of finding employment after graduation. Additionally, connections made during an internship can provide valuable referrals and recommendations. Strong relationships with supervisors and colleagues often lead to positive references that can bolster a resume and support job applications. These references can be critical when applying for positions, as they offer potential employers a trusted assessment of the candidate's abilities, work ethic, and fit for the role. Personal recommendations from industry professionals can carry significant weight and enhance a candidate's credibility in the job market.

Networking with industry professionals also provides access to insider knowledge about job openings and career opportunities. Many positions are filled through word-of-mouth and internal referrals rather than public job postings. By maintaining relationships with professionals in their field, interns can gain early access to job leads and opportunities that might not be widely advertised. This insider knowledge can give them a competitive edge and help them secure positions that align with their career goals. Beyond immediate job prospects, professional connections play a crucial role in long-term career development. The relationships formed during an internship can lead to ongoing mentorship and guidance. Mentors and industry contacts can provide valuable career advice, share insights into industry trends, and offer support as one navigates their professional journey. This guidance can be instrumental in making informed career decisions, setting goals, and navigating challenges that arise throughout one's career. Moreover, networking during an internship can facilitate opportunities for professional growth and development. Connections with professionals in the field can lead to invitations to industry events, conferences, and workshops. These events provide additional learning opportunities and a platform to further expand one's network. Attending such events can enhance one's knowledge of industry trends, provide exposure to new ideas and technologies, and create additional opportunities for career advancement. Building a robust professional network also increases visibility within the industry. By staying connected with colleagues and industry professionals, interns can ensure that they remain on the radar of potential employers and collaborators. This visibility can lead to opportunities for involvement in projects, partnerships, or initiatives that align with their career interests. It also helps in establishing a personal brand and reputation within the industry, which can be beneficial for career advancement. Furthermore, connections made during an internship can serve as a source of inspiration and motivation. Interacting with successful professionals can provide insights into different career paths and highlight various opportunities that one might not have previously considered. These interactions can also foster a sense of community and support, helping interns to stay motivated and focused on their career aspirations. The importance of professional connections made during an internship extends far beyond the immediate benefits of gaining experience and skills. These connections can significantly influence future job opportunities, provide valuable referrals, offer insider knowledge about job openings, and facilitate long-term career development. They also contribute to professional growth, visibility within the industry, and personal motivation. By investing time and effort into building and maintaining these relationships, interns can enhance their career prospects and set a strong foundation for future success.

1.4. Resume Building

- **A well-crafted resume:** A well-crafted resume is a powerful tool for securing employment and advancing one's career, and internships offer a prime opportunity to build and refine this essential document. Internships provide a platform for gaining practical experience, acquiring new skills, and making professional connections—all of which are critical elements to highlight on a resume. Crafting an effective resume during and after an internship involves more than simply listing duties and responsibilities; it requires a strategic approach to showcase achievements, skills, and experiences in a manner that aligns with career goals and the expectations of potential employers. One of the primary benefits of an internship is the hands-on experience it provides. This experience is invaluable for resume building, as it demonstrates practical application of knowledge and skills acquired through academic study. Interns should carefully document their responsibilities and achievements during the internship, focusing on specific tasks they handled and any projects they contributed to. This detailed documentation should highlight not only what they did but also the impact of their contributions. For example, instead of simply stating "assisted with marketing campaigns," a more effective description would be "developed and implemented social media marketing strategies that increased engagement by 30%." Quantifying achievements is a crucial aspect of resume building. Numbers and percentages provide concrete evidence of success and effectiveness, making the resume more compelling to potential employers. Interns should strive to include measurable outcomes related to their work. This could involve anything from the number of projects completed, the percentage increase in performance metrics, or the scale of an event managed. These quantifiable results offer tangible proof of the intern's capabilities and the value they brought to the organization. In addition to detailing specific responsibilities and accomplishments, a resume should reflect the skills acquired during the internship. These skills might include technical competencies, such as proficiency with software or tools relevant to the industry, as well as soft skills like communication, teamwork, and problem-solving. Interns should identify and articulate these skills clearly on their resumes, providing examples of how they applied them in real-world scenarios. For instance, if an intern improved team collaboration through effective communication strategies, this should be highlighted as a key soft skill, accompanied by a brief explanation of how this contributed to project success. Another important aspect of resume building during an internship is the inclusion of relevant projects and contributions. Interns should list any significant projects they were involved in, describing their role and the outcomes achieved. Projects that showcase initiative, leadership, or innovation are particularly valuable. For example, if an intern led a project to streamline a process that resulted in a 20% reduction in time spent on administrative tasks, this should be prominently featured. Detailing such projects demonstrates the intern's ability to apply their skills effectively and contribute to organizational goals. Professional experiences gained through an internship can also be leveraged to demonstrate industry knowledge and expertise. Interns should emphasize their understanding of industry-specific practices, tools, and trends. This could include familiarity with industry standards, regulatory requirements, or emerging technologies. Highlighting this knowledge shows potential employers that the intern is not only experienced but also well-versed in the nuances of the industry. Networking and professional connections made during the internship can also play a role in resume building. While these connections themselves are not typically listed on a resume, the experiences and endorsements they provide can enhance the resume's content. For example, positive feedback or recommendations from supervisors and colleagues can be referenced in a cover letter or during job interviews, adding credibility to the claims made on the resume. Interns should consider requesting letters of recommendation or endorsements that can be included in their job application materials or referenced in their resume. The structure and formatting of the resume are equally important. A well-organized resume with a clear, professional format ensures that key information is easily accessible to potential employers. Interns should use a clean, modern design with distinct sections such as experience, skills, education, and projects. Each section should be clearly labeled and formatted consistently. Bullet points can be used to list achievements and responsibilities succinctly, making it easy for readers to scan the document quickly. Additionally, using action verbs and precise language helps to convey the intern's contributions effectively. Interns should also tailor their resume to the specific job or industry they are targeting. This involves adjusting the resume to highlight the most relevant experiences and skills for each application. Customizing the resume ensures that it aligns with the requirements and expectations of the potential employer, increasing the likelihood of being noticed and considered for the position. This targeted approach shows that the intern has carefully considered how their background fits with the job and is prepared to contribute meaningfully. Building a strong resume during an internship involves more than simply listing job duties; it requires a thoughtful approach to documenting achievements, quantifying results, highlighting skills, and showcasing relevant projects and industry knowledge. By effectively leveraging the experiences and skills gained during an internship, interns can create a compelling resume that enhances their employability and sets them apart in a competitive job market. A well-crafted resume not only reflects the intern's capabilities but also demonstrates their readiness to contribute effectively to future employers.

- **Experience Highlighting:** Internships add practical experience to a resume, making candidates more attractive to future employers. Experience highlighting during an internship is a critical aspect of translating hands-on experience into tangible benefits for future career opportunities. The ability to effectively showcase and articulate what was learned and achieved during an internship can significantly enhance an intern's resume and professional profile. This process involves not only documenting daily tasks but also emphasizing the skills developed, the impact of contributions, and the overall value added to the organization. Highlighting experience effectively requires a strategic approach to ensure that the most relevant and impressive aspects of the internship are communicated clearly and compellingly. One key element of experience highlighting is identifying and emphasizing significant achievements. Rather than merely listing routine tasks, it is crucial to focus on accomplishments that had a measurable impact. For example, if an intern was involved in a project that improved a process or increased efficiency, detailing the results of these efforts provides concrete evidence of their contribution. Quantifying achievements, such as by stating that a marketing campaign led to a 25% increase in engagement or that a data analysis project reduced errors by 15%, offers tangible proof of the intern's effectiveness and skill level. These specific examples make a stronger impression on potential employers than general descriptions of job duties. Another important aspect of highlighting experience is showcasing the development of new skills and competencies. Internships often provide opportunities to acquire and refine both technical and soft skills. Technical skills might include proficiency in industry-specific software, tools, or methodologies, while soft skills might encompass communication, teamwork, and problem-solving abilities. Interns should identify which skills they developed or enhanced during their internship and provide examples of how these skills were applied in practical situations. For instance, if an intern improved their ability to manage projects effectively, describing how they organized and led a team through a complex project demonstrates their growing competency in this area. Experience highlighting also involves illustrating how the intern's role contributed to broader organizational goals. Interns should articulate how their work supported the objectives of their team or department and how it aligned with the organization's mission. This perspective not only shows an understanding of the bigger picture but also highlights the intern's ability to contribute meaningfully to organizational success. For example, if an intern worked on a project that contributed to the development of a new product or service, explaining how this project fit into the company's strategic goals helps demonstrate the intern's awareness of and impact on the organization's direction. Effective communication of experience also requires presenting the work in a context that is relevant to potential future employers. Interns should tailor the way they highlight their experiences to align with the job roles they are targeting. This involves emphasizing aspects of the internship that are most relevant to the desired position or industry. For example, if an intern is applying for a role in project management, they should focus on experiences that involved project planning, team coordination, and execution. This tailored approach ensures that the highlighted experiences are directly applicable to the job in question and demonstrates the intern's preparedness for the role. In addition to documenting achievements and skills, it is also beneficial to reflect on personal growth during the internship. This includes identifying areas where the intern has expanded their knowledge, improved their work habits, or developed a greater understanding of their field. Personal growth can be highlighted by discussing specific instances where the intern overcame challenges, adapted to new environments, or took initiative. These reflections offer a deeper insight into the intern's journey and can help potential employers understand how the internship experience has shaped their professional development. Networking and building relationships during the internship also contribute to experience highlighting. Positive interactions with colleagues, mentors, and supervisors can lead to valuable endorsements and recommendations. When discussing experience on a resume or in interviews, referencing feedback or support from these professional connections can add credibility to the intern's achievements. Testimonials or letters of recommendation from supervisors can further validate the intern's contributions and skills, providing additional weight to their highlighted experiences. Furthermore, experience highlighting should include a focus on specific projects or tasks that required creativity, leadership, or innovation. Projects that demonstrate the intern's ability to think outside the box or lead a team effectively can be particularly compelling. For example, if an intern developed a new strategy that led to measurable improvements, detailing this project showcases not only their technical skills but also their strategic thinking and leadership capabilities. These types of experiences often stand out to employers and can differentiate an intern from other candidates. Experience highlighting during an internship involves more than just listing tasks and responsibilities; it requires a strategic approach to showcasing significant achievements, skills developed, and contributions to organizational goals. By quantifying results, tailoring experiences to relevant job roles, reflecting on personal growth, and leveraging professional connections, interns can effectively communicate their value and readiness for future career opportunities. Properly highlighting these experiences can significantly enhance a resume and professional profile, setting the stage for success in the competitive job market.

- **Accomplishments:** Interns can showcase specific achievements and contributions made during their internship, demonstrating their capabilities. Accomplishments during an internship are critical markers of professional growth and value addition that can significantly impact future career opportunities. Internships provide a unique environment for applying theoretical knowledge in real-world scenarios, and the achievements made in this context can serve as compelling evidence of one's capabilities and potential. Effectively documenting and showcasing these accomplishments is essential for building a strong professional profile and enhancing employability. One of the most impactful ways to highlight accomplishments is through quantifiable results. Interns should focus on achievements that can be measured in concrete terms, such as improvements in performance metrics, successful project completions, or increased efficiencies. For example, if an intern played a key role in a marketing campaign that resulted in a 20% increase in customer engagement, this specific metric provides clear evidence of the intern's contribution and effectiveness. Quantifying accomplishments in this way not only makes them more impressive but also helps potential employers understand the tangible impact the intern has had. Accomplishments should also reflect the intern's initiative and problem-solving abilities. Internships often present challenges that require creative solutions or proactive approaches. Highlighting instances where the intern identified a problem and developed an effective solution demonstrates critical thinking and resourcefulness. For instance, if an intern noticed inefficiencies in a workflow and proposed a new system that streamlined processes, detailing this accomplishment shows an ability to contribute positively and drive improvements. Such achievements indicate that the intern is not just performing tasks but actively contributing to the organization's success. Another important aspect of showcasing accomplishments is demonstrating leadership and teamwork. Even in entry-level or support roles, there are opportunities to lead projects, coordinate with team members, and contribute to group objectives. Interns who take on leadership roles, whether formal or informal, and successfully guide projects or teams highlight their ability to manage responsibilities and work collaboratively. For example, if an intern led a cross-departmental team to complete a project ahead of schedule, this accomplishment reflects strong leadership and organizational skills. Showcasing these experiences emphasizes the intern's capacity to handle increased responsibilities and work effectively within a team. Innovation and creativity are also crucial elements of accomplishments. Interns who introduce new ideas or approaches that positively impact their work environment demonstrate an ability to think outside the box. Whether it's developing a new process, creating a unique marketing strategy, or implementing a novel solution to a recurring problem, such achievements illustrate a proactive and inventive mindset. Highlighting these accomplishments shows potential employers that the intern is not only capable of executing existing tasks but also of contributing original ideas and improvements. Effective communication and presentation of accomplishments are key to making them stand out. Interns should ensure that their achievements are clearly articulated in resumes, cover letters, and interviews. Using action verbs and specific details helps to convey the significance of the accomplishments. For instance, rather than simply stating "worked on a project," a more effective description would be "spearheaded a project to develop a new client onboarding system, resulting in a 30% reduction in onboarding time." This level of detail provides a clearer picture of the intern's role and the impact of their contributions. Moreover, accomplishments should be aligned with career goals and the job being applied for. Tailoring the presentation of achievements to highlight experiences and skills that are most relevant to the desired position can make a significant difference. For example, if applying for a role in data analysis, emphasizing accomplishments related to data management, analysis projects, or insights gained from data will be particularly relevant. This tailored approach ensures that the highlighted accomplishments resonate with potential employers and align with their expectations. In addition to individual accomplishments, it is valuable to recognize and mention collaborative successes. Achievements that result from teamwork or collective efforts demonstrate the intern's ability to work effectively with others and contribute to shared goals. For instance, if an intern was part of a team that successfully launched a new product, detailing the role played in the team's success and the outcomes achieved provides a comprehensive view of their contributions. Reflection on personal growth during the internship also adds depth to the discussion of accomplishments. Interns should consider how their experiences have contributed to their professional development, such as improving specific skills, gaining new insights, or overcoming challenges. This reflection not only highlights the value of the internship experience but also shows a commitment to personal and professional growth. Effectively highlighting accomplishments during an internship involves focusing on quantifiable results, demonstrating initiative and problem-solving abilities, showcasing leadership and teamwork, and emphasizing innovation and creativity. Clear communication and presentation of these achievements, aligned with career goals, are crucial for building a compelling professional profile. By strategically documenting and articulating these accomplishments, interns can create a strong foundation for future career opportunities and stand out in a competitive job market.

1.5. Skill Enhancement

- **Transferable Skills:** Interns develop skills that are valuable in any career, such as communication, teamwork, and problem-solving. Transferable skills developed during an internship are fundamental assets that can significantly influence career advancement and professional success. These skills, which include both technical and soft skills, are valuable across various roles and industries, making them crucial for long-term career development. Internships provide a practical environment where these skills can be cultivated and demonstrated, offering a foundation for future employment opportunities and professional growth. Technical skills acquired during an internship are often industry-specific but can have broader applications depending on the field. For example, an intern working in a marketing role might develop proficiency in data analysis, social media management, or content creation. These technical competencies are essential for the specific role but can also be applicable in other marketing positions or even in different industries that require similar skills. Similarly, technical skills such as project management, research methodologies, or proficiency with certain software tools can be valuable in various professional settings. Documenting these skills and highlighting their application during the internship helps to build a versatile skill set that enhances employability across multiple fields. Beyond technical abilities, soft skills developed during an internship are highly transferable and crucial for career success. These include communication, teamwork, problem-solving, time management, and adaptability. Effective communication, for instance, is vital in nearly every professional context. Interns often have opportunities to present ideas, write reports, or collaborate with colleagues, which hones their ability to convey information clearly and professionally. This skill is essential not only in job interviews but also in daily workplace interactions, making it a key component of professional effectiveness. Teamwork is another critical transferable skill. Interns frequently work as part of a team, contributing to group projects and collaborating with colleagues from diverse backgrounds. This experience teaches interns how to function effectively within a team, handle conflicts, and leverage the strengths of others. The ability to work well with others is a universally valuable skill that employers highly seek, as it directly impacts productivity and project outcomes.

Demonstrating effective teamwork in various contexts, whether through collaborative projects or interdepartmental initiatives, highlights an intern's capacity to contribute to and enhance team dynamics. Problem-solving skills are developed as interns encounter and address various challenges during their work. Interns may be tasked with finding solutions to operational issues, improving processes, or navigating unexpected obstacles. These experiences cultivate a problem-solving mindset and the ability to approach complex situations analytically. Employers value candidates who can think critically, identify problems, and develop effective solutions, making problem-solving a crucial transferable skill. Providing examples of how problems were addressed and resolved during the internship showcases this skill in action and its potential application in future roles. Time management is another important skill that internships help develop. Balancing multiple tasks, meeting deadlines, and managing competing priorities are common challenges faced during an internship. Learning to organize and prioritize work effectively not only improves productivity but also prepares interns for the demands of a professional environment. Effective time management skills are applicable across all industries and job functions, making them essential for career progression. Interns should highlight instances where they successfully managed their workload, met deadlines, or efficiently handled multiple responsibilities to demonstrate their proficiency in this area. Adaptability is increasingly important in today's fast-paced and ever-changing work environments. Interns often face evolving project requirements, shifting priorities, or new technologies, which require flexibility and the ability to adjust quickly. Developing adaptability during an internship helps interns become resilient and open to change, qualities that are highly valued by employers. Examples of how interns navigated changes or adapted to new situations can illustrate their ability to thrive in dynamic environments and tackle new challenges effectively. To maximize the impact of transferable skills, interns should focus on clearly articulating these skills on their resumes, cover letters, and in interviews. Providing specific examples and demonstrating how these skills were applied during the internship helps to validate their relevance and effectiveness. For instance, rather than simply stating "strong communication skills," an intern might describe how they successfully led a presentation or facilitated a team meeting. Such examples provide concrete evidence of the skill in action and its value to potential employers. Moreover, transferable skills developed during an internship can be leveraged to explore diverse career paths and opportunities. For instance, a skill such as project management can be relevant in various roles, from marketing to operations to consulting. Interns who recognize the versatility of their skills and are able to apply them in different contexts are better positioned to adapt to various job roles and industries. This adaptability not only broadens career options but also enhances long-term career resilience and growth. Transferable skills gained during an internship are invaluable assets that enhance career prospects and professional development. Technical skills, such as proficiency with industry-specific tools, along with soft skills like communication, teamwork, problem-solving, time management, and adaptability, are crucial for success in various professional settings. Effectively documenting and articulating these skills, and providing specific examples of their application, can significantly boost an intern's employability and career path. By leveraging these transferable skills, interns can build a strong foundation for future career opportunities and navigate a diverse range of professional paths.

- **Industry-Specific Skills:** Interns gain hands-on experience with tools, technologies, and methodologies specific to their field. During an internship, industry-specific skills play a crucial role in bridging the gap between theoretical knowledge and real-world application. These skills are tailored to the particular demands and nuances of a specific field, providing interns with hands-on experience that is directly relevant to their chosen industry. Mastering these skills not only enhances the intern's proficiency in their area of interest but also significantly boosts their employability by demonstrating a practical understanding of the industry's standards and practices. One of the primary benefits of developing industry-specific skills during an internship is the opportunity to gain practical experience with the tools and technologies used in the field. For instance, an intern in a technology-focused role might learn to work with specific programming languages, software platforms, or development environments that are prevalent in the tech industry. Similarly, an intern in a finance role might gain experience with financial modelling software, data analysis tools, or industry-standard financial practices. This hands-on experience with relevant tools and technologies not only solidifies the intern's technical expertise but also makes them more attractive to potential employers who are seeking candidates with practical, applied skills. Moreover, internships provide a unique environment to learn and apply industry-specific methodologies and practices. Each industry has its own set of standards, procedures, and best practices that are essential for success. For example, an intern in a marketing role might learn about specific campaign strategies, market research techniques, and branding guidelines that are crucial for effective marketing. In contrast, an intern in the healthcare sector might become familiar with clinical protocols, patient management systems, and healthcare regulations. Understanding and implementing these methodologies during an internship equips the intern with the knowledge and experience required to navigate the industry's unique challenges and expectations. Industry-specific skills also encompass an understanding of the sector's regulatory and compliance requirements. Many industries have specific regulations and standards that professionals must adhere to, and internships often provide insight into these requirements. For instance, an intern in the legal field might gain experience with legal research methods, case management systems, and compliance with legal standards. In contrast, an intern in environmental science might learn about regulatory compliance related to environmental protection and sustainability. Familiarity with these regulations ensures that interns can operate effectively within the industry's legal and ethical frameworks, an important aspect that prospective employers highly value. Networking and relationship-building are also integral to developing industry-specific skills during an internship. Interns often interact with professionals who have extensive experience and knowledge in the field. These interactions provide opportunities to learn from seasoned experts, gain insights into industry trends, and understand the nuances of working in the industry. Networking within the industry can also lead to mentorship opportunities, where experienced professionals offer guidance and advice based on their own experiences. Building relationships with industry insiders not only enhances the intern's understanding of the field but also opens doors for future career opportunities and professional growth. Another significant aspect of industry-specific skills is the ability to apply theoretical knowledge to practical situations. Internships often involve working on real-world projects, solving industry-specific problems, and participating in day-to-day operations. This practical application helps interns to see how their academic learning translates into actionable skills and outcomes. For example, an intern in a business consulting firm might use strategic analysis techniques learned in their coursework to address client challenges, while an intern in a design studio might apply design principles to create visual content for real clients. This experiential learning reinforces the relevance of their academic background and demonstrates their ability to apply knowledge effectively in a professional setting. Understanding industry trends and staying current with emerging developments is another crucial component of industry-specific skills. Internships often expose interns to the latest trends, technologies, and innovations in their field. Being aware of these trends allows interns to contribute to forward-thinking projects and adapt to evolving industry demands. For instance, an intern in the technology sector might work on projects involving artificial intelligence or cybersecurity, gaining experience with cutting-edge technologies. In contrast, an intern in the fashion industry might be involved in projects related to sustainable fashion or digital design. Staying abreast of industry trends ensures that interns remain relevant and competitive in their field. Furthermore, industry-specific skills often include developing a deep understanding of the sector's target audience or market. Interns learn about the needs, preferences, and behaviours of the industry's key stakeholders, which informs their work and helps them make more strategic decisions. For example, an intern in the consumer goods industry might study consumer behaviour and preferences to help develop effective marketing strategies, while an intern in the non-profit sector might gain insight into the needs of various communities to better support fundraising and outreach efforts. Understanding the target audience is essential for creating effective solutions and making meaningful contributions to the organization. Industry-specific skills developed during an internship are pivotal for translating academic knowledge into practical expertise and enhancing employability. These skills encompass proficiency with relevant tools and technologies, understanding industry methodologies and regulations, networking with professionals, applying theoretical knowledge to real-world scenarios, staying current with industry trends, and understanding the target audience. By focusing on these skills during an internship, interns not only gain valuable experience but also position themselves as knowledgeable and capable candidates in their chosen field. This combination of practical experience and industry-specific expertise is crucial for achieving career success and advancing in a competitive job market.

1.6. Academic Credit

- **Educational Requirements:** Some internships are part of academic programs and offer credit towards graduation. This can provide a structured learning experience aligned with academic goals. Educational requirements for internships are a fundamental aspect of the internship experience, serving as both a prerequisite for participation and a guide for the skills and knowledge that interns are expected to bring to the role. These requirements often reflect the academic background needed to perform effectively in the internship and can vary significantly depending on the industry, role, and organization. Understanding and meeting these educational prerequisites is essential for securing an internship and maximizing the learning experience. Internships typically require a specific level of education, which often correlates with the complexity of the tasks and responsibilities assigned. For many internships, particularly those in technical or specialized fields, organizations expect candidates to have completed relevant coursework or hold a degree in a related discipline. For instance, an internship in engineering might require candidates to be pursuing or have completed a degree in engineering or a closely related field, while an internship in finance may require coursework in economics, accounting, or financial analysis. This educational background ensures that interns have a foundational understanding of key concepts and principles that they can apply in their role. In addition to formal degree requirements, internships often require specific coursework or academic achievements. For example, an internship in a research lab might require candidates to have completed coursework in scientific research methods or to have achieved a certain GPA in relevant subjects. This requirement ensures that interns are equipped with the necessary theoretical knowledge and academic skills to contribute effectively to research projects or technical tasks. Meeting these educational requirements demonstrates to potential employers that the intern has a solid academic foundation and is prepared to handle the responsibilities of the internship. Educational requirements can also include particular certifications or specializations relevant to the field. In some industries, additional certifications or specialized training can be prerequisites for securing an internship. For example, an internship in information technology might require candidates to have certifications in specific programming languages or software applications. Similarly, an internship in health care might require specific certifications or training related to patient care or medical procedures. These certifications and specializations validate the intern's expertise and preparedness for the role, highlighting their commitment to their chosen field and their readiness to undertake specialized tasks. The relevance of educational requirements to the internship role is crucial. Internships are designed to provide practical experience that complements academic learning, so it is essential that the educational background of candidates aligns with the nature of the work they will be doing. For instance, a marketing internship might require coursework in marketing principles, consumer behavior, or digital media strategies, ensuring that the intern can apply theoretical concepts to real-world marketing campaigns. Similarly, an internship in graphic design might require proficiency in design software and an understanding of design theory, as indicated by relevant coursework or a portfolio of work. This alignment ensures that interns can contribute meaningfully to projects and gain valuable experience in their field. Meeting educational requirements also facilitates the intern's ability to engage with and benefit from the mentorship and training provided during the internship. Interns who have a strong academic background are better positioned to understand complex concepts, grasp new skills quickly, and contribute to projects with minimal additional training. This readiness not only enhances the intern's learning experience but also makes them a more valuable asset to the organization. Organizations often seek interns who can integrate quickly and contribute effectively, and meeting the educational prerequisites is a key factor in achieving this goal. Educational requirements also serve as a benchmark for evaluating potential candidates. They help organizations identify individuals who possess the foundational knowledge and skills necessary to succeed in the internship. This evaluation process ensures that candidates are equipped to handle the demands of the role and are likely to benefit from the internship experience. For candidates, meeting these requirements demonstrates their qualifications and suitability for the position, making them more competitive in the application process. Additionally, understanding and fulfilling educational requirements can guide prospective interns in their academic and career planning. Knowing the specific educational prerequisites for internships in their desired field can help students make informed decisions about their coursework, specializations, and extracurricular activities. For example, a student interested in a finance internship might choose to focus on courses in financial modeling and analysis or seek out additional certifications in finance to align with industry expectations. This strategic approach to education ensures that students are well-prepared for internship opportunities and can maximize their career prospects. Educational requirements for internships are critical in ensuring that candidates have the necessary academic background, knowledge, and skills to succeed in their roles. These requirements often include specific degrees, coursework, certifications, and specializations relevant to the field. Meeting these prerequisites not only demonstrates a candidate's readiness and suitability for the internship but also enhances their ability to contribute effectively and benefit from the experience. Understanding and adhering to educational requirements helps candidates align their academic pursuits with career goals, ultimately facilitating a more successful and rewarding internship experience.

1.7. Confidence Building

- **Professional Development:** Gaining experience and achieving success in a real-world setting helps build confidence in one's abilities and career potential. Confidence building and professional development are crucial aspects of an internship experience, as they play a significant role in shaping an intern's career path and overall professional growth. Cultivating confidence and pursuing continuous professional development not only enhance an intern's immediate effectiveness but also lay the foundation for long-term career success. Confidence building during an internship is an essential process that impacts various aspects of a professional's growth. Interns often start their roles with a mix of excitement and apprehension. Building confidence involves overcoming initial uncertainties and gradually becoming more assured in one's abilities and contributions. As interns gain experience and receive positive feedback, they begin to feel more capable and self-reliant. This growing confidence helps them take on more challenging tasks, engage more actively in discussions, and assert their ideas with greater conviction. One key factor in confidence building is the successful completion of tasks and projects. As interns accomplish their goals and meet objectives, they experience a sense of achievement that bolsters their self-esteem. Each successful project or positive feedback from supervisors reinforces the intern's belief in their abilities, encouraging them to tackle more complex responsibilities. This cycle of setting goals, achieving them, and receiving validation creates a positive feedback loop that strengthens confidence. Another important element of confidence building is receiving constructive feedback and mentorship. Interns who actively seek feedback from supervisors and colleagues can gain valuable insights into their performance and areas for improvement. Constructive feedback helps interns understand their strengths and weaknesses, enabling them to make targeted improvements. Positive reinforcement and mentorship further enhance confidence by affirming the intern's progress and potential. Mentors can provide guidance, support, and encouragement, helping interns to navigate challenges and develop a more robust sense of self-assurance. Networking and building relationships within the organization also contribute to confidence building. Interacting with professionals, attending meetings, and participating in team activities allow interns to gain visibility and establish a presence. Building a network of supportive colleagues and mentors provides a sense of belonging and validation, which can boost confidence. Being part of a professional community helps interns feel more integrated and valued, reinforcing their belief in their own capabilities. In parallel with confidence building, professional development is a continuous process that involves acquiring new skills, expanding knowledge, and gaining experience. Internships offer a unique opportunity for professional development by providing hands-on experience in a real-world setting. Interns can apply academic learning to practical situations, develop technical skills, and learn industry-specific practices. This practical experience is invaluable for bridging the gap between theoretical knowledge and real-world application. Professional development during an internship also includes the opportunity to refine soft skills, such as communication, teamwork, and problem-solving. Interns often work on collaborative projects, engage in discussions, and interact with various stakeholders, which helps them develop and enhance these essential skills. Effective communication and teamwork are critical for professional success, as they contribute to successful project outcomes and positive work relationships. By honing these skills during their internship, interns are better prepared for the demands of their future careers. Another key aspect of professional development is exposure to industry trends and best practices. Interns have the opportunity to observe and learn about the latest developments in their field, including emerging technologies, industry standards, and organizational practices. This exposure helps interns stay informed about industry advancements and equips them with knowledge that is relevant to their career. Staying current with industry trends enhances an intern's ability to contribute effectively and make informed decisions. Mentorship and guidance are integral components of professional development. Interns who work closely with experienced professionals can benefit from their insights, advice, and support. Mentors can provide valuable feedback, help interns navigate their roles, and offer guidance on career planning. This mentorship fosters professional growth and helps interns develop a clearer understanding of their career path and goals. Networking is also a crucial aspect of professional development. Building a network of professional contacts allows interns to gain visibility, learn from industry experts, and explore potential career opportunities. Networking can lead to mentorship opportunities, job referrals, and valuable connections that can support career advancement. Engaging with professionals in the field helps interns build relationships and gain insights that can shape their career. Professional development involves setting and pursuing career goals. Internships provide a platform for interns to explore their interests, identify their strengths, and set career objectives. By reflecting on their experiences and assessing their goals, interns can make informed decisions about their career path and take proactive steps toward achieving their aspirations. This goal-oriented approach helps interns stay focused and motivated, contributing to their overall professional growth. Confidence building and professional development are integral to a successful internship experience. Confidence is developed through achieving goals, receiving feedback, and building relationships, which enhances an intern's self-assurance and effectiveness. Professional development involves acquiring practical skills, refining soft skills, staying informed about industry trends, benefiting from mentorship, and networking. Together, these elements contribute to a well-rounded and fulfilling internship experience, preparing interns for future career success and growth.

- **Independence:** Interns often take on responsibilities that require self-management and initiative, fostering independence. Independence is a cornerstone of the internship experience, allowing interns to cultivate essential skills in self-management and initiative. As interns transition from academic environments to professional settings, they frequently encounter responsibilities that require them to operate autonomously, make decisions, and manage their own tasks. This shift not only enhances their ability to work independently but also prepares them for future roles in their careers. In an internship, the ability to manage oneself effectively is a crucial skill that often emerges from taking on various responsibilities. Interns are typically assigned specific projects or tasks that necessitate a certain degree of independence. For instance, an intern might be tasked with conducting research, preparing reports, or managing parts of a project, all of which require them to take initiative and work without constant supervision. This responsibility pushes interns to develop a strong sense of accountability and self-discipline as they navigate their roles and deliver results. The experience of managing tasks independently also helps interns to hone their problem-solving skills. Without immediate oversight, interns must identify issues, devise solutions, and execute their plans. This process fosters critical thinking and decision-making abilities, as interns learn to assess situations, weigh options, and make informed choices. For example, if an intern encounters a challenge with a project, they need to independently determine the best course of action to resolve the issue, whether it involves seeking additional information, consulting resources, or devising a new strategy. Developing independence also involves managing time effectively. Interns often juggle multiple responsibilities and deadlines, requiring them to prioritize tasks and allocate their time efficiently. This aspect of self-management is crucial for maintaining productivity and meeting expectations. Interns learn to create schedules, set goals, and manage their workload in a way that ensures timely completion of their tasks. By mastering time management, interns not only enhance their efficiency but also build a foundation for managing more complex responsibilities in future roles. Taking initiative is another key aspect of fostering independence. Interns are often encouraged to go beyond their assigned duties, propose new ideas, and contribute proactively to projects. This proactive approach demonstrates their willingness to engage with their work and make meaningful contributions. For instance, an intern might identify a potential improvement in a process or suggest a new approach to a project based on their observations and insights. By taking initiative, interns show their ability to think creatively and drive positive changes within the organization. The development of independence during an internship also involves learning to navigate organizational dynamics and workplace relationships. Interns must interact with various stakeholders, including supervisors, colleagues, and clients, while managing their own responsibilities. This requires them to communicate effectively, manage expectations, and collaborate with others while maintaining their own focus and objectives. Building these skills helps interns to adapt to different work environments and to work independently while still being part of a team. Furthermore, independence during an internship often involves a degree of self-reflection and self-assessment. Interns are encouraged to evaluate their own performance, identify areas for improvement, and set personal goals. This reflective practice helps them to understand their strengths and weaknesses, develop a growth mindset, and take ownership of their professional development. By regularly assessing their progress and seeking feedback, interns can continuously refine their skills and enhance their independence. The experience of working independently also prepares interns for the demands of future careers. Many professional roles require individuals to take initiative, manage their own tasks, and make decisions without constant oversight. Interns who develop strong independent work habits during their internships are better equipped to handle these responsibilities in their future roles. This experience not only boosts their confidence but also demonstrates their readiness for more advanced positions and challenges. In addition to its practical benefits, fostering independence during an internship contributes to personal growth and self-reliance. Interns who successfully manage their own tasks and take initiative gain a sense of accomplishment and self-efficacy. This personal growth extends beyond the workplace, as the skills developed through independent work—such as problem-solving, time management, and proactive thinking—are applicable in various aspects of life. Independence is a critical component of the internship experience, encompassing self-management, initiative, and personal growth. Interns are given responsibilities that require them to operate autonomously, make decisions, and manage their own tasks. This experience fosters critical thinking, time management, problem-solving, and proactive behavior, preparing them for future career challenges and personal development. By developing these skills, interns not only enhance their effectiveness in their current roles but also build a strong foundation for success in their future careers.

1.8. Potential for Employment

- **Job Offers:** Internships can lead to full-time job offers from the same organization if the intern demonstrates strong performance and a good fit with the company culture. Internships are often viewed as a stepping stone to full-time employment, providing valuable opportunities for interns to transition into permanent roles within the same organization. When an intern demonstrates strong performance and aligns well with the company culture, the internship can serve as a gateway to a job offer, offering a direct path to continued employment and career advancement. A successful internship can lead to a full-time job offer when an intern consistently exhibits high performance and contributes positively to the organization. Interns who demonstrate a strong work ethic, achieve their goals, and deliver results are likely to be noticed by their supervisors. Their ability to handle responsibilities effectively and their dedication to their work create a positive impression, which can influence the decision to offer them a permanent position. Interns who excel in their roles often become valuable assets to the team, showcasing skills and qualities that the organization may wish to retain long-term. In addition to performance, alignment with the company culture plays a significant role in the potential for receiving a job offer. Organizations often seek individuals who not only possess the necessary skills but also fit well with the company's values, work environment, and team dynamics. Interns who integrate seamlessly into the organizational culture, display a positive attitude, and collaborate effectively with colleagues are more likely to be seen as a good fit. Demonstrating enthusiasm for the company's mission and adapting well to the work environment can make an intern a strong candidate for a full-time position. The experience of working within the organization during an internship provides both the intern and the employer with a unique opportunity to assess mutual compatibility. Interns gain insight into the company's operations, culture, and expectations, while the organization evaluates the intern's performance, skills, and fit with the team. This two-way assessment helps ensure that if a job offer is extended, it is based on a well-informed understanding of how the intern will contribute to the organization in a permanent role. Additionally, the internship period allows interns to build relationships and network within the organization. By working closely with colleagues, supervisors, and other stakeholders, interns can establish a professional network and create connections that can support their transition to full-time employment. Building these relationships helps interns to become more integrated into the team and increases their visibility within the organization, further enhancing their chances of receiving a job offer. Furthermore, demonstrating a proactive attitude and a willingness to take on additional responsibilities can also contribute to the likelihood of receiving a job offer. Interns who go beyond their assigned tasks, seek out new opportunities, and contribute to projects in a meaningful way show initiative and a strong commitment to the organization. This proactive behavior signals to employers that the intern is motivated and eager to contribute, qualities that are often highly valued in potential full-time employees. The feedback and evaluations provided during the internship also play a crucial role in determining whether a job offer will be extended. Regular performance reviews and feedback sessions give interns the opportunity to understand their strengths and areas for improvement. By addressing feedback constructively and making continuous improvements, interns can enhance their performance and demonstrate their readiness for a full-time role. Positive feedback from supervisors and colleagues can further reinforce the decision to offer a permanent position. Internships can lead to full-time job offers when interns demonstrate strong performance and a good fit with the company culture. By excelling in their roles, aligning with organizational values, and integrating well into the team, interns increase their chances of receiving a permanent job offer. The internship period provides both the intern and the organization with valuable insights into their compatibility, allowing for an informed decision about future employment. Proactive behavior, strong relationships, and constructive responses to feedback further contribute to the likelihood of transitioning from an internship to a full-time position, making the internship experience a crucial step toward long-term career success.

- **Reference Letters:** Positive feedback from supervisors during an internship can lead to strong reference letters, which are valuable for future job applications. Reference letters play a significant role in the internship experience, offering both benefits to interns and valuable insights to potential future employers. These letters, typically written by supervisors, mentors, or colleagues, serve as formal endorsements of the intern's skills, work ethic, and overall contributions during the internship. They provide a detailed account of the intern's performance and character, which can be instrumental in shaping their career prospects. During an internship, the opportunity to receive a reference letter is a key benefit, as it provides a written record of the intern's achievements and abilities. A well-crafted reference letter highlights the intern's specific contributions, strengths, and accomplishments, offering a concrete endorsement of their performance. This written testimonial can significantly enhance an intern's resume and job applications by providing prospective employers with credible, third-party validation of their skills and work ethic. Reference letters offer a personalized perspective on the intern's abilities, as they are tailored to reflect the intern's unique experiences and achievements. Unlike generic resumes or cover letters, reference letters provide specific examples and detailed observations from individuals who have directly supervised or worked closely with the intern. This personalized approach helps potential employers gain a clearer understanding of the intern's capabilities and the value they can bring to a future role. For instance, a reference letter might detail how an intern successfully managed a complex project, demonstrated strong leadership skills, or contributed to a team effort, offering concrete evidence of their qualifications. Furthermore, reference letters serve as a valuable tool for building credibility and trust with future employers. A positive reference from a respected professional or supervisor can greatly enhance an intern's job prospects, as it provides reassurance to potential employers about the intern's suitability for the role. Employers often rely on reference letters to verify the information provided in resumes and interviews, and a strong endorsement can help an intern stand out in a competitive job market. A reference letter that highlights the intern's strengths and achievements can also reinforce the positive impression made during the interview process, further boosting their chances of securing a job. In addition to their role in job applications, reference letters can also support career development and professional growth. For example, they can be used when applying for further educational opportunities, such as graduate programs or specialized training. Educational institutions and programs often require reference letters as part of the application process, and a strong letter from an internship supervisor can enhance the intern's application by showcasing their relevant skills and experiences. Similarly, reference letters can be valuable for securing professional certifications or membership in industry organizations, as they provide evidence of the intern's competencies and professional achievements. The process of obtaining a reference letter also offers valuable insights and feedback for interns. Requesting and receiving a reference letter often involves discussions with supervisors or mentors about the intern's performance and achievements. These conversations provide an opportunity for interns to reflect on their experiences, receive constructive feedback, and gain a better understanding of their strengths and areas for improvement. This feedback can be instrumental in guiding future career decisions and professional development efforts. To maximize the benefits of reference letters, interns should approach the request process thoughtfully. It is important to choose individuals who are familiar with the intern's work and can provide a detailed and positive assessment. When requesting a reference letter, interns should provide their references with ample information about their accomplishments, roles, and responsibilities during the internship, ensuring that the letter reflects their most significant achievements. Providing a well-organized list of accomplishments and contributions can help the reference writer craft a comprehensive and impactful letter. Reference letters are a crucial component of the internship experience, offering substantial benefits for both the intern and their future career prospects. They provide personalized endorsements of the intern's skills and performance, enhancing their credibility and job applications. Reference letters also support career development by contributing to applications for further education and professional opportunities. By thoughtfully requesting and utilizing reference letters, interns can leverage these endorsements to build their professional reputation, gain valuable feedback, and advance their careers effectively.

CHAPTER TWO

Different Types of Internships

Internships come in a variety of types, each offering different kinds of experiences and opportunities. Internships may be paid, unpaid, part-time, full-time etc. Understanding the different types of internships can help individuals choose the opportunity that best aligns with their professional aspirations and educational background.

2.1. Paid Internships: Internships where the intern receives financial compensation for their work. These internships are often found in fields like finance, technology, and engineering, where organizations have the resources to offer salaries or stipends. Paid internships not only help interns gain professional experience but also provide financial support, making them an attractive option for many students and recent graduates.

Benefits of Paid Internships

- **Financial Support:**Helps cover living expenses and other costs.
- **Increased Motivation:** Often leads to higher levels of engagement and commitment.
- **Competitive Advantage:** Paid internships can attract a wider range of applicants and are typically seen as more prestigious. Like corporate finance internships, software development internships at tech companies, marketing internships.

2.2. Unpaid Internships: Internships where the intern does not receive financial compensation. These internships are prevalent in fields such as non-profits, arts, and media, where funding may be limited. Although unpaid, these internships often offer substantial learning experiences and can lead to significant career benefits, including mentorship, industry exposure, and potential future job opportunities.

Benefits of unpaid Internships

- **Experience and Learning:** Provides valuable experience and skill development.
- **Opportunities in Nonprofits:** Often found in nonprofit organizations or smaller startups where funding is limited.
- **Example:** Internships at non-profit organizations, academic research internships, internships in small businesses.

2.3. Full-Time Internships: Internships where the intern works full-time hours, typically 35-40 hours per week.

Benefits of Full Time Internships

- **Immersive Experience:** Provides a more comprehensive experience in the organization.
- **Greater Responsibilities:** Often involves more significant projects and responsibilities.

2.4. Part-Time Internships: Internships where the intern works fewer hours, usually 10-20 hours per week. Part-time internships are designed for students or professionals who may be balancing other commitments, such as coursework or a current job.

Benefits of Part Time Internships

- **Flexibility:** Allows interns to balance work with other commitments, such as coursework or part-time jobs.
- **Ongoing Experience:** Can be spread over a longer period, providing continuous learning.
- **Example:** Internships during the academic semester, internships that accommodate part-time study.

2.5. Remote Internships: Virtual internships, or remote internships, offer the flexibility of working from any location, often through digital communication tools and online platforms. These internships have become increasingly popular, especially in fields like technology and digital marketing. Virtual internships provide the advantage of flexible schedules and the ability to work with organizations regardless of geographical constraints, though they may require strong self-discipline and effective remote communication skills. Internships conducted virtually, allowing interns to work from any location.

Benefits of Remote Internships

- **Flexibility:** Offers the convenience of working from home or any location.
- **Broader Opportunities:** Enables participation with organizations located in different geographic areas.
- **Self-Discipline:** Requires strong self-management and communication skills.
- **Example:** Digital marketing internships, remote software development internships, virtual research assistant positions.

2.6. Academic Internships: Internships that are part of an academic program and often provide academic credit. Academic internships are integrated into academic programs and are typically required or recommended as part of a degree curriculum. These internships are structured to provide students with practical experience related to their field of study, often accompanied by academic credit. They are designed to bridge the gap between classroom learning and real-world application, helping students apply theoretical knowledge in a professional setting.

Benefits of Academic Internships

- **Structured Learning:** Aligns with academic objectives and can integrate coursework with practical experience.

- **Academic Credit:** Contributes towards degree requirements and can often be a mandatory component of the program.
- **Example:** Internships arranged through university career services, co-op programs, internships for credit.

2.7. Co-op Programs: Cooperative education programs that integrate work experience with academic study, often alternating between academic terms and work terms. Co-op internships are similar to academic internships but usually involve a more extended period of work, often alternating between full-time work and academic study. Co-op programs are typically more immersive, allowing students to gain in-depth industry experience over a longer duration. These internships provide a comprehensive understanding of the field and can enhance job prospects by offering substantial work experience.

Benefits of Co-op Programs

- **Extended Experience:** Provides in-depth, extended periods of work experience.
- **Educational Integration:** Blends academic learning with practical application.
- **Example:** Engineering co-op programs, business co-op placements.

2.8. Project-Based Internships: Internships focused on completing a specific project or set of tasks.

Benefits of Project-Based Internships

- **Focused Experience:** Allows interns to concentrate on a particular area or project.
- **Clear Goals:** Provides a structured, goal-oriented experience.
- Internships involving research projects, marketing campaigns, product development.

2.9. Micro-Internships: Short-term internships that often last a few weeks or involve a specific task or project.

Benefits of Micro-Internships

- **Short-Term Commitment:** Ideal for those looking to gain quick experience or explore new fields without a long-term commitment.
- **Specific Focus:** Allows interns to work on specific projects or tasks.
- **Example:** Summer projects, seasonal tasks, short-term assignments.

2.10. Summer internships: Summer internships are a popular and valuable opportunity for students and recent graduates to gain practical experience and enhance their career prospects during the summer months. These internships typically take place during the summer break from school or university, making them an ideal option for those looking to focus on gaining professional experience without the distractions of coursework. Summer internships are often full-time positions, providing interns with an immersive experience in their chosen field. This full-time commitment allows interns to engage deeply with their roles, take on significant projects, and contribute meaningfully to their organizations. The concentrated period of work—usually spanning between 8 to 12 weeks—offers interns a comprehensive understanding of the industry and the chance to develop their skills extensively within a relatively short timeframe.

Benefits of Summer Internships

- One of the primary benefits of summer internships is the opportunity to apply classroom knowledge in a real-world setting. Students and recent graduates can take the theories and concepts they have learned in their academic studies and see how they are applied in a professional context. This hands-on experience not only reinforces their learning but also helps them understand how their skills and knowledge translate into practical work scenarios.

- Summer internships also provide valuable networking opportunities. Interns have the chance to connect with professionals in their field, attend industry events, and build relationships that can be beneficial for their future careers. Networking during a summer internship can lead to mentorship opportunities, job referrals, and a better understanding of industry trends and practices. The connections made during these internships often play a crucial role in shaping future career paths and opening doors to potential job opportunities.

- Summer internships often serve as a gateway to full-time employment. Many organizations use summer internships as a talent pipeline, evaluating interns for potential future roles within the company. Interns who demonstrate strong performance, a good fit with the company culture, and a proactive attitude may be offered full-time positions upon graduation. This transition from intern to employee is a common outcome for successful summer internships, providing a smooth path from academic studies to professional employment.

- For students, summer internships can also help clarify career goals and interests. By working in a specific industry or role, interns gain firsthand experience that helps them assess whether it aligns with their career aspirations. This exposure can be instrumental in making informed decisions about future career paths, choosing a major, or pursuing further education.

- Furthermore, summer internships provide an opportunity to build and enhance various skills that are crucial for professional success. Interns can develop technical skills relevant to their field, improve their problem-solving abilities, and enhance their communication and teamwork skills. The experience of working on real projects, collaborating with colleagues, and receiving feedback helps interns build a strong skill set that can be highlighted in future job applications and interviews. Summer internships offer a wealth of benefits for students and recent graduates. They provide a full-time, immersive experience that bridges academic learning with practical application, allowing interns to develop valuable skills and gain industry insight. The opportunity to network, explore career interests, and potentially secure future employment further enhances the value of summer internships. By participating in these internships, individuals can significantly advance their professional development and set a strong foundation for their future careers.

2.11. International Internships: Internships conducted in a country outside of the intern's home country.

Benefits of International Internships

- **Global Experience:** Provides exposure to international work environments and cultures.
- **Language Skills:** Opportunity to improve language skills and understand global industry practices.
- **Example:** Internships with multinational corporations, international development internships.

CHAPTER THREE

Benefits of Internships

Interns can be benefited with the internships in several ways. Their professional growth; skills development, networking opportunities, personal growth; confidence building, time management, & Industry insights and real-world experience are the way to their success. Internships offer a multitude of benefits, serving as a crucial bridge between academic learning and professional experience. They provide practical exposure to the workplace, allowing individuals to apply theoretical knowledge in real-world settings. This hands-on experience is invaluable for developing a deep understanding of industry practices and refining skills that are essential for career success. One of the primary advantages of internships is the opportunity for professional growth and skill development. Interns gain practical experience that enhances their resumes and builds their expertise in specific fields. This experience often includes acquiring technical skills, learning to navigate workplace dynamics, and developing soft skills such as communication, teamwork, and problem-solving. Such skills are critical for future job performance and can significantly enhance an individual's employability. Internships also offer valuable networking opportunities. By working alongside professionals, interns have the chance to build relationships with industry experts, mentors, and peers. These connections can provide guidance, career advice, and potential job referrals. Networking during an internship can open doors to future employment opportunities and help individuals stay informed about industry trends and developments. Furthermore, internships provide insight into career paths and help clarify professional interests. Interns gain a clearer understanding of what a particular role or industry entails, which can inform their career choices and educational decisions. This exposure helps individuals assess whether a specific career aligns with their goals and interests, leading to more informed decisions about their future. In addition to these practical benefits, internships often serve as a stepping stone to full-time employment. Many organizations use internships as a means to evaluate potential future employees. Interns who perform well and fit in with the company culture may receive job offers upon graduation. This direct pathway from internship to full-time employment can provide a seamless transition into the workforce and significantly boost career prospects.

3.1 Career Exploration

- **Understanding Various Job Roles**
  Internships provide insight into different roles within a company or industry, helping interns explore various career options. An intern at a large corporation might rotate through different departments, gaining a comprehensive view of potential career paths.
- **Assessing Career Fit**
  By experiencing a role firsthand, interns can assess whether it aligns with their career aspirations and personal interests. Like an intern interested in graphic design might discover a passion for UX/UI design after working on related projects.
- **Gaining Insight into Industry Trends**
  Internships offer exposure to current industry trends

and practices, keeping interns informed about the latest developments. Like an intern in the fashion industry might learn about emerging trends and technologies that are shaping the future of fashion.

3.2 Networking Opportunities

- **Building Professional Relationships**
  Internships provide opportunities to connect with professionals, peers, and mentors in the industry. For example, Interns might attend industry events or meetings, where they can build relationships with influential figures and future colleagues.
- **Access to Mentorship and Guidance**
  Many internships offer mentorship from experienced professionals who can provide valuable career advice and feedback. An intern may receive regular feedback from their supervisor, helping them improve their skills and navigate their career path.
- **Expanding Professional Connections**
  Networking during internships can lead to future job opportunities and professional collaborations. An intern who makes a strong impression may be recommended for future job openings or professional projects.

3.3 Resume Building

- **Highlighting Relevant Experience**
  Internships add practical experience to a resume, making candidates more attractive to potential employers. An intern who worked on a significant

project can list specific achievements and responsibilities, showcasing their capabilities.

- **Demonstrating Achievements and Contributions**
  Interns can highlight concrete achievements and contributions made during their internship. An intern who contributed to a successful marketing campaign can include metrics and results in their resume.

- **Differentiating from Other Candidates**
  Relevant internship experience can set candidates apart from others with similar academic qualifications. A candidate with internship experience in a highly competitive field may stand out compared to other applicants without such experience.

3.4 Skill Enhancement

- **Developing Transferable Skills**
  Internships help develop skills that are valuable across various industries, such as communication, teamwork, and problem-solving. An intern working in a team environment improves their ability to collaborate effectively with others.

- **Acquiring Industry-Specific Knowledge**
  Interns gain knowledge and skills specific to their industry, which can be crucial for future career success. A finance intern learns about financial modeling and analysis techniques used in the finance sector.

- **Improving Communication and Teamwork**
  Internships provide opportunities to enhance communication skills and work effectively in team settings. Interns often participate in team meetings and collaborative projects, honing their ability to

communicate and work with others.

3.5 Academic Credit and Integration

- **Earning Academic Credit through Internships**
  Some internships are part of academic programs and offer credit towards graduation, integrating practical experience with academic learning. A university may offer credit for internships that align with a student's major, allowing them to fulfill degree requirements.
- **Integrating Academic Learning with Practical Experience**
  Internships help students apply theoretical knowledge in a real-world context, enhancing their educational experience. A business intern might apply principles learned in business management courses to real-world business challenges.
- **Enhancing Educational Outcomes**
  Internships can enhance educational outcomes by providing hands-on experience that complements classroom learning. Students who participate in internships often report a deeper understanding of their field and improved academic performance.

3.6 Confidence Building

- **Gaining Self-Efficacy through Real-World Experience**
  Internships help build confidence by allowing individuals to succeed in real-world scenarios and apply their skills effectively. Successfully completing challenging projects during an internship can boost an

intern's confidence in their abilities.

- **Developing Independence and Initiative**
Interns often take on responsibilities that require them to work independently and take initiative. An intern who leads a project or manages a task develops independence and a proactive attitude.

- **Overcoming Professional Challenges**
Internships provide opportunities to tackle real-world challenges, helping interns build resilience and problem-solving skills. An intern who navigates complex tasks or solves problems learns to handle challenges and adapt to changing situations.

3.7 Potential for Employment

- **Securing Full-Time Job Offers**
Many internships lead to full-time job offers if interns demonstrate strong performance and fit well with the company culture. A company may offer a full-time position to an intern who has proven their value and contributed significantly to the organization.

- **Gaining Strong References and Recommendations**
Positive feedback from supervisors during an internship can result in strong references and recommendations for future job applications. An intern who receives a glowing recommendation from a supervisor can use it to strengthen their job applications.

- **Increasing Employability and Marketability**
Internships enhance employability by providing relevant experience and skills that make candidates more attractive to employers. Interns with industry-specific experience are often more competitive in the

job market compared to those without such experience.

3.8 Personal Growth

- **Fostering Professional and Personal Development**
  Internships contribute to both professional and personal development, helping individuals grow in various aspects of their lives. Interns may develop a stronger sense of professionalism and better work habits through their experiences.
- **Enhancing Problem-Solving and Adaptability**
  Internships provide opportunities to tackle problems and adapt to new situations, enhancing problem-solving and adaptability skills. An intern who handles unexpected challenges learns to think on their feet and adapt to changing circumstances.
- **Building a Strong Work Ethic**
  Internships help individuals develop a strong work ethic, including reliability, responsibility, and dedication. Consistently meeting deadlines and performing well in an internship fosters a strong work ethic that benefits future career endeavours.

CHAPTER FOUR

Finding the Right Internship

Finding the right internship involves a strategic approach to ensure that the opportunity aligns with your career goals, interests, and skills. The process of finding an ideal internship begins with a clear understanding of what you hope to achieve from the experience and then systematically exploring opportunities that match those objectives. To start, it is essential to define your goals and interests. Consider what skills you want to develop, the industry you wish to explore, and the type of work environment that suits you best. Reflect on your long-term career aspirations and how an internship could help you achieve them. This clarity will guide your search and help you identify internships that offer relevant experiences and opportunities for growth. Next, research potential organizations and industries that align with your interests. Utilize various resources, including career services at your educational institution, online job boards, professional networking sites like LinkedIn, and industry-specific websites. These platforms often list available internships and provide information about the organizations offering them. Pay attention to the descriptions of internship roles, required qualifications, and the nature of the work to ensure they match your career goals and interests. Networking plays a crucial role in finding the right internship. Engage with professionals in your field of interest through informational interviews, career fairs, and industry events. Building relationships with industry experts and alumni can provide valuable insights and lead to potential internship opportunities that may not be advertised publicly. Additionally, reaching out to professors or mentors who have connections in your desired field can also be beneficial. When evaluating internship opportunities, consider factors such as the organization's reputation, the scope of the internship role, and the learning objectives. Look for internships that offer meaningful work and align with your skills and interests, rather than roles that merely provide administrative tasks. A well-structured internship should offer you opportunities to contribute to real projects, work alongside experienced professionals, and gain practical experience relevant to your career goals. It is also important to assess the logistics of the internship, including location, duration, and compensation. Determine whether the internship is feasible based on your personal circumstances, such as your availability and financial situation. For instance, if you are seeking a paid internship to support your expenses, ensure that the roles you apply for offer financial compensation. Similarly, if you prefer a remote or part-time internship due to other commitments, look for opportunities that accommodate those needs.

4.1. Self-Assessment

4.1.1. Identify Your Goals

- **Career Objectives:** Determine what you want to achieve in your career. Are you looking to gain experience in a specific field, develop particular skills, or explore different career paths?
- **Skill Development:** Assess the skills you want to develop or improve. This can help you find internships that align with your learning objectives.

4.1.2. Evaluate Your Interests

- **Industry Preferences:** Reflect on the industries or sectors you're passionate about.
- **Job Roles:** Consider the types of roles or job functions that intrigue you.

4.1.3. Assess Your Skills and Strengths

- **Technical Skills:** Identify any technical skills you have that are relevant to potential internships.
- **Soft Skills:** Consider your strengths in communication, teamwork, problem-solving, and other soft skills.

4.2. Research Potential Internships
4.2.1. Explore Industries and Companies

- **Industry Research:** Look into various industries to understand which ones align with your interests and goals.
- **Company Research:** Identify companies known for their internship programs, company culture, and values.

4.2.2. Utilize Online Resources

- **Job Boards:** Use platforms like LinkedIn, Indeed, Glassdoor, and other job boards to search for internship opportunities.
- **Company Websites:** Visit the career sections of companies you're interested in to find internship listings.

4.2.3. Leverage University Resources

- **Career Services:** Take advantage of your school's career services for internship listings and advice.
- **Alumni Networks:** Connect with alumni who may provide insights or opportunities in your field of interest.

4.3. Networking
4.3.1. Build Professional Relationships

- **Industry Events:** Attend industry conferences, seminars, and workshops to meet professionals and learn about internship opportunities.
- **Networking Groups:** Join professional associations or groups related to your field.

4.3.2. Utilize Social Media

- **LinkedIn:** Connect with industry professionals, join relevant groups, and follow companies that interest you.
- **Twitter and Other Platforms:** Follow industry leaders and organizations for updates on internship openings.

4.3.3. Informational Interviews

- **Conduct Interviews:** Arrange informational interviews with professionals in your field to learn more about their career paths and potential internship opportunities.

4.4. Apply Strategically
4.4.1. Tailor Your Application Materials

- **Resume:** Customize your resume to highlight relevant skills and experiences for each internship you apply for.
- **Cover Letter:** Write personalized cover letters that explain why you're interested in the specific internship and how you can contribute.

4.4.2. Prepare for Interviews

- **Research:** Learn about the company's mission, values, and recent projects.
- **Practice:** Prepare for common interview questions and practice discussing your skills and experiences.

4.4.3. Follow Up

- **Application Status:** Follow up with employers after submitting your application or interview to express continued interest and inquire about the status of your application.

4.5. Evaluate Internship Offers
4.5.1. Consider the Fit

- **Role and Responsibilities:** Ensure that the role and responsibilities align with your career goals and interests.

- **Company Culture:** Evaluate whether the company culture and values are a good fit for you.

4.5.2. Assess Compensation and Benefits

- **Financial Compensation:** If applicable, consider the financial compensation and whether it meets your needs.
- **Additional Benefits:** Look into other benefits such as mentorship, networking opportunities, and professional development.

4.5.3. Think Long-Term

- **Future Opportunities:** Consider whether the internship may lead to future employment opportunities or provide valuable connections in your industry.
- **Skill Development:** Assess whether the internship offers the opportunity to develop or enhance the skills you're seeking.

4.6. Tips for Success
4.6.1. Stay Organized

- **Track Applications:** Keep a record of the internships you've applied for, including deadlines, contact information, and follow-up actions.
- **Set Goals:** Set clear goals for your internship search and application process to stay focused and motivated.

4.6.2. Be Persistent

- **Apply Widely:** Apply to multiple internships to increase your chances of finding the right fit.
- **Learn from Rejections:** Use any feedback from rejections to improve your applications and interview skills.

4.6.3. Seek Advice

- **Mentors and Advisors:** Seek guidance from mentors, career advisors, or professors who can provide valuable insights and advice.

CHAPTER FIVE

Application Process

The application process for an internship involves several stages, each designed to present your qualifications and fit for the role effectively. The application process for internships often involves submitting a resume, cover letter, and sometimes additional materials such as portfolios or references. Tailor these documents to highlight your relevant experiences, skills, and enthusiasm for the specific role. A well-crafted resume and cover letter that clearly demonstrate your fit for the internship can significantly enhance your chances of securing an interview. Prepare for interviews by researching the organization and the role thoroughly. Understand the company's mission, values, and recent developments, and be ready to articulate how your background and goals align with their needs. Practicing common interview questions and scenarios will help you present yourself confidently and professionally. Start by exploring various sources such as job boards, company websites, career services at your educational institution, and professional networking sites. Look for internships that match your career interests and academic background. Pay close attention to the descriptions of the roles, the skills required, and the organization's culture. This research will help you target opportunities that are aligned with your career aspirations and ensure that your application is well-tailored to each role. Your resume should be carefully crafted to highlight your relevant skills, experiences, and achievements. Tailor your resume to emphasize the aspects of your background that align with the internship role. Use specific examples to demonstrate your accomplishments and the skills you bring to the table. The cover letter is another critical component of your application. It should complement your resume by providing a more detailed narrative of your qualifications and explaining why you are interested in the internship and how you fit with the organization's needs. Your cover letter should be personalized for each application, addressing the specific requirements of the role and showing your enthusiasm for the opportunity. Highlight your relevant experiences, your understanding of the company's mission, and how you can contribute to their goals. After submitting your application materials, you may be invited for an interview. Preparation is key for a successful interview. Research the organization thoroughly to understand its mission, values, and recent developments. Prepare answers to common interview questions and be ready to discuss your experiences and how they relate to the internship role. Practice articulating your strengths, accomplishments, and career goals in a clear and confident manner. Additionally, prepare thoughtful questions to ask the interviewer about the internship, the team, and the organization. During the interview, it is important to demonstrate not only your qualifications but also your enthusiasm and fit for the role. Show your interest in the company by discussing how its values and mission align with your own. Be proactive in highlighting how your skills and experiences make you a strong candidate for the internship. Effective communication, professionalism, and a positive attitude are crucial in making a strong impression. After the interview, follow up with a thank-you note to express your appreciation for the opportunity and to reinforce your interest in the internship. A well-crafted thank-you note can help you stand out and leave a positive impression with the interviewer. Use this opportunity to reiterate your enthusiasm for the role and briefly highlight why you are a great fit.

5.1. Self-Assessment and Preparation

5.1.1. Clarify Your Goals

- **Career Objectives:** Define what you want to achieve from the internship, such as gaining experience in a specific field, developing new skills, or exploring different career paths.
- **Desired Outcomes:** Consider what kind of role or responsibilities you are looking for in the internship.

5.1.2. Prepare Application Materials

- **Resume:** Update your resume to highlight relevant skills, experiences, and achievements. Tailor it for each internship application to emphasize aspects that align with the job description.
- **Cover Letter:** Write a personalized cover letter for each internship application. Address it to the appropriate person, if possible, and explain why you're interested in the role and how your skills and experiences make you a strong candidate.
- **Portfolio:** If relevant (e.g., for design, writing, or other creative fields), prepare a portfolio showcasing your work and achievements.

5.2. Research and Identify Opportunities
5.2.1. Explore Internship Opportunities

- **Job Boards and Websites:** Use platforms like LinkedIn, Indeed, Glassdoor, and specialized internship sites to search for internships.
- **Company Websites:** Visit the career sections of companies you're interested in to find available internships.
- **University Resources:** Utilize your school's career services and internship databases.

5.2.2. Evaluate Opportunities

- **Job Description:** Review the responsibilities and qualifications required for each internship to ensure they align with your career goals and skills.
- **Company Research:** Research the company's mission, values, culture, and recent projects to determine if it's a good fit for you.

5.3. Application Submission
5.3.1. Tailor Your Application

- **Resume Customization:** Adapt your resume to match the skills and qualifications outlined in the job description. Highlight relevant experiences and accomplishments.
- **Cover Letter Personalization:** Craft a cover letter that addresses the specific internship and company. Use it to demonstrate your enthusiasm, relevant skills, and how you can contribute to the organization.

5.3.2. Follow Application Instructions

- **Submission Method:** Follow the application instructions precisely, whether submitting through an online portal, via email, or through a university career center.
- **Documents Required:** Ensure you include all required documents, such as a resume, cover letter, transcripts, or any other materials specified in the job listing.

5.3.3. Application Tracking

- **Record Applications:** Keep a record of all the internships you've applied for, including application dates, submission methods, and any follow-up actions required.

5.4. Interview Preparation
5.4.1. Research the Company

- **Company Information:** Learn about the company's history, mission, values, and recent news. Understanding the company's culture and recent developments will help you in interviews.
- **Role-Specific Knowledge:** Familiarize yourself with the role's requirements and how your background aligns with them.

5.4.2. Practice Common Interview Questions

- **Behavioral Questions:** Prepare for questions about your past experiences, how you handle challenges, and how you work in teams.

- **Situational Questions:** Be ready to discuss how you would handle hypothetical situations related to the role.

5.4.3. Prepare Questions for the Interviewer

- **Insightful Questions:** Prepare thoughtful questions to ask the interviewer about the internship, team dynamics, company culture, and expectations.

5.4.4. Mock Interviews

- **Practice:** Conduct mock interviews with friends, mentors, or career advisors to practice your responses and receive feedback.

5.5. Interview Process
5.5.1. First Round Interviews

- **Format:** These might be conducted over the phone, via video call, or in person. Be prepared for initial screening questions and basic evaluations of your fit for the role.

5.5.2. Second Round Interviews

- **In-Depth Evaluation:** These interviews typically involve more detailed questions about your skills, experiences, and how you handle specific situations. You may also meet with team members or supervisors.

5.5.3. Assessments and Exercises

- **Skills Tests:** Some internships may require you to complete tests or exercises related to the role, such as coding challenges, case studies, or writing samples.

5.6. Follow-Up
5.6.1. Thank You Notes

- **Send a Thank You Email:** After the interview, send a thank you note to express your appreciation for the opportunity to interview. Reiterate your interest in the position and mention something specific from the interview.

5.6.2. Inquire About Next Steps

- **Follow-Up:** If you haven't heard back within the timeframe provided, follow up with a polite email to inquire about the status of your application.

5.7. Evaluating Offers
5.7.1. Review the Offer

- **Role and Responsibilities:** Ensure the role aligns with your goals and interests.
- **Compensation and Benefits:** Assess the salary (if applicable), benefits, work hours, and other relevant details.

5.7.2. Negotiate if Necessary

- **Discuss Terms:** If needed, negotiate aspects of the offer, such as compensation, start date, or work arrangements.

5.7.3. Accept or Decline

- **Formal Acceptance:** If you choose to accept the offer, confirm your acceptance in writing and complete any required paperwork.
- **Inform Other Employers:** Notify other companies where you've applied or interviewed of your decision.

5.8. Preparing for the Internship
5.8.1. Onboarding

- **Documentation:** Complete any required paperwork or documentation before starting.
- **Preparation:** Familiarize yourself with the company's policies, procedures, and tools you'll be using.

5.8.2. Set Goals

- **Learning Objectives:** Identify what you hope to achieve during the internship and set specific, measurable goals.

5.8.3. Orientation

- **Company Culture:** Participate in any orientation or training sessions to understand the company culture and expectations.

CHAPTER SIX

Intern Project Ideas

Creating meaningful and impactful intern projects is essential for maximizing the benefits of internships for both organizations and interns. By selecting the best intern project ideas that align with business objectives, match intern skills, and provide clear objectives and support, companies can ensure successful outcomes. Internships with well-designed projects not only enhance the learning experience for interns but also contribute to the organization's growth and success. One of the key types of intern projects involves process improvement. Interns can be tasked with analyzing existing workflows or systems and identifying areas for enhancement. For example, an intern might be assigned to review the efficiency of a company's inventory management system. They could use data analysis tools to pinpoint bottlenecks, propose changes to streamline operations, and develop a plan for implementing these improvements. This type of project allows interns to apply their problem-solving skills, gain experience in process optimization, and contribute to increased operational efficiency. Another valuable intern project idea is market research and analysis. Interns can be involved in researching market trends, customer preferences, and competitive landscape. For instance, an intern might be asked to conduct a survey to gather feedback on a new product or service. They could then analyze the results and present insights on how the company might adjust its marketing strategy or product features to better meet customer needs. This type of project helps interns develop their research and analytical skills, while also providing the company with actionable data to inform strategic decisions. Content creation and management is another area where interns can make significant contributions. Interns can work on developing content for the company's website, blog, or social media platforms. They might be responsible for writing articles, creating graphics, or producing videos that align with the company's brand and messaging. For example, an intern might create a series of blog posts on industry trends or develop a social media campaign to promote an upcoming event. This project helps interns build their content creation skills and provides the company with fresh, engaging material for its digital presence. Project management is a practical and educational project idea for interns. Interns can be given the responsibility of leading or supporting specific projects within the organization. They might assist in planning and executing a marketing campaign, organizing an internal event, or managing a product development phase. For instance, an intern could be tasked with coordinating the logistics of a company-wide meeting, including scheduling, communications, and materials preparation. This experience allows interns to develop project management skills, learn about team coordination, and understand the complexities of managing tasks and deadlines. Customer service and support projects can also be valuable for interns. They can work on improving customer service processes or developing new support tools. An intern might be involved in analyzing customer feedback, identifying common issues, and proposing solutions to enhance the customer experience. For example, they could create a comprehensive FAQ section for the company's website based on common customer inquiries or develop a guide for handling customer complaints more effectively. This type of project helps interns gain experience in customer relations and contributes to improved service quality. Data analysis and reporting is another area where interns can contribute significantly. Interns can be tasked with gathering, analyzing, and reporting on various data sets to support business decisions. For example, an intern might analyze sales data to identify trends and create reports that highlight key performance indicators. They could use data visualization tools to present their findings in a clear and actionable format. This project helps interns develop their data analysis skills and provides valuable insights to the organization. Creative problem-solving projects can also be highly effective. Interns can be assigned to tackle specific challenges or come up with innovative solutions to existing problems. For instance, an intern might be tasked with developing a new approach to streamline internal communications or proposing a strategy to improve employee engagement. This type of project encourages creative thinking and allows interns to demonstrate their problem-solving abilities. Community outreach and engagement projects offer interns the chance to work on initiatives that enhance the company's social responsibility efforts. Interns might help organize volunteer events, develop partnerships with local organizations, or create campaigns to raise awareness about social issues. For example, an intern could coordinate a company-wide charity drive or develop a proposal for a new community engagement program. This project not only supports the company's corporate social responsibility goals but also allows interns to contribute to meaningful causes. Intern projects are an essential component of the internship experience, offering valuable learning opportunities and contributing to the organization's objectives. Whether focused on process improvement, market research, content creation, project management, customer service, data analysis, creative problem-solving, or community outreach, well-designed projects provide interns with practical experience and help them develop key skills. By selecting projects that align with both the intern's strengths and the organization's needs, companies can maximize the impact of their internship programs and support the professional growth of their interns.

6.1 Development of an effective intern project involves

- **Identifying Organizational Needs:** Identify the key areas where interns can make a meaningful contribution, considering current challenges and opportunities.
- **Matching Projects with Intern Skills:** Assign projects that match the interns' skills and interests to ensure they are engaged and can perform well.
- **Defining Clear Objectives and Deliverables:** Set clear objectives and deliverables for the projects to provide direction and a basis for evaluating success.
- **Providing Necessary Resources and Support:** Ensure interns have access to the necessary tools, resources, and support to complete their projects effectively.
- **Setting Up Regular Check-Ins and Feedback Loops:** Make sure to have regular check-ins to keep track of

how things are going, give feedback, and deal with any problems that come up.

- **Evaluating Project Outcomes:** Assess the outcomes of the projects to measure their impact and identify areas for improvement.

6.2. Benefits of Well-Designed Intern Projects

Well-designed intern projects offer numerous benefits for both the organization and the interns.

6.2.1 For the Organization

- **Fresh Perspectives and Innovative Ideas:** Interns can introduce fresh ideas and viewpoints that inspire innovation and creativity in the company.
- **Talent Pipeline Development:** Internships can serve as a talent pipeline, allowing organizations to identify and recruit top talent for future positions.

6.2.2 For the Intern

- **Practical Experience and Skill Development:** Interns learn by doing and pick up important skills that can help them in their future careers.
- **Professional Growth and Networking Opportunities:** Interns also get chances to grow professionally and meet people who can help them in their careers.

6.3 Intern Project Ideas for Different Categories

6.3.1 Research and Analysis Projects

1. **Conduct market research to identify new opportunities.**

2. Analyze competitor strategies and market positioning.
3. Evaluate customer feedback to improve products/ services.
4. Research industry trends and emerging technologies.
5. Analyze financial data to identify cost-saving opportunities.

6.3.2 Technology and Development Projects

6. Develop a new feature for a mobile application.
7. Design and implement a website redesign project.
8. Create a prototype for a new software solution.
9. Optimize database performance and data management.
10. Automate manual processes using scripting or coding.

6.3.3 Marketing and Social Media Projects

11. Develop and execute a social media marketing campaign.
12. Create engaging content for blogs, social media, and newsletters.
13. Conduct keyword research and implement SEO strategies.
14. Analyze marketing metrics to optimize campaign performance.
15. Develop a brand awareness campaign targeting a specific audience.

6.3.4 Operations and Process Improvement Projects

16. Streamline workflow processes to improve efficiency.

17. Implement inventory management software for better tracking.
18. Conduct a supply chain analysis to identify bottlenecks.
19. Improve customer service processes to enhance satisfaction.
20. Implement quality control measures to ensure product consistency.

6.3.5 Creative and Design Projects

21. Design graphics for marketing materials and presentations.
22. Produce videos highlighting company culture or products.
23. Create branding guidelines to maintain visual consistency.
24. Develop interactive user interfaces for web or mobile applications.
25. Design packaging concepts for new product launches.

6.3.6 Data Analysis and Visualization Projects

26. Analyze sales data to identify trends and patterns.
27. Create dashboards for monitoring key performance indicators.
28. Conduct sentiment analysis on customer feedback data.
29. Visualize survey results using charts and graphs.
30. Develop predictive models to forecast future trends.

6.3.7 Environmental Sustainability Projects

31. Conduct an energy audit to identify opportunities for conservation.
32. Implement recycling programs to reduce waste.
33. Research eco-friendly alternatives for packaging materials.
34. Analyze water usage and implement conservation measures.
35. Develop a sustainability report outlining environmental initiatives.

6.3.8 Community Engagement Projects

36. Organize a volunteer event or community service project.
37. Create educational materials on social or environmental issues.
38. Develop partnerships with local organizations for outreach programs.
39. Plan and execute fundraising events for a charitable cause.
40. Implement a mentorship program for underprivileged youth.

6.3.9 Diversity and Inclusion Projects

41. Conduct diversity training sessions for employees.
42. Develop recruitment strategies to attract diverse candidates.
43. Implement policies to promote inclusivity in the workplace.
44. Create affinity groups for employees from underrepresented backgrounds.

45. Organize cultural awareness events to celebrate diversity.

6.3.10 Health and Wellness Projects

46. Implement a workplace wellness program promoting physical activity.
47. Develop resources for mental health awareness and support.
48. Conduct ergonomic assessments to improve workstation setups.
49. Create resources for stress management and work-life balance.

CHAPTER SEVEN

Making the Most of Your Internship

Making the most of your internship involves actively engaging in your role, seeking out opportunities for growth, and leveraging the experience to advance your career. Majorly it involves setting goals and expectations, Building relationships with mentors and colleagues, and seeking feedback and acting on it. First and foremost, set clear goals for what you want to achieve during the internship. Reflect on your career aspirations and identify specific skills or experiences you want to gain. Communicate these goals with your supervisor to ensure alignment and to gain their support in achieving them. Having clear objectives will help you focus your efforts, make informed decisions about your tasks, and track your progress throughout the internship. Actively seek out and take on meaningful projects that align with your goals. Don't wait for tasks to be assigned; instead, express your interest in taking on additional responsibilities and contribute to projects that interest you. Volunteering for challenging assignments not only demonstrates initiative but also allows you to gain valuable experience and showcase your abilities. Engage with various aspects of the organization to broaden your understanding and skills. Building relationships with colleagues is another crucial aspect of making the most of your internship. Take the time to network within the organization by introducing yourself to team members and participating in team meetings and events. Establishing connections with colleagues and mentors can provide you with valuable insights, feedback, and opportunities for future collaboration. It also helps you integrate into the team and understand the organizational culture better. Effective communication is key to maximizing your internship experience. Maintain open lines of communication with your supervisor and seek regular feedback on your performance. Ask questions if you're unsure about tasks or need guidance. Constructive feedback is essential for growth, and addressing any issues promptly can help you stay on track and improve your performance. Additionally, keep your supervisor informed about your progress and any accomplishments, as this helps them recognize your contributions. Demonstrate a strong work ethic and professionalism in all your interactions. Show up on time, meet deadlines, and approach your work with enthusiasm and a positive attitude. Being reliable and committed to your tasks reflects well on you and can lead to increased responsibilities and recognition within the organization. Professionalism also involves adhering to company policies and practices, which helps you integrate smoothly into the workplace. Take the initiative to learn beyond your assigned tasks. Explore other departments, attend company events, and engage in any available training or development opportunities. This proactive approach allows you to gain a broader perspective on the organization and industry, enhancing your overall experience. By actively seeking out learning opportunities, you can develop new skills and gain a deeper understanding of the field. Document your achievements and experiences throughout the internship. Keep a record of the projects you work on, the skills you develop, and any positive feedback you receive. This documentation will be valuable for updating your resume and preparing for future job applications or interviews. Reflecting on your experiences also helps you assess what you've learned and how it aligns with your career goals. Finally, make sure to express your gratitude and appreciation for the opportunity. A thank-you note to your supervisor and colleagues can go a long way in leaving a positive impression and maintaining professional relationships. Acknowledging the support and guidance you received during your internship demonstrates professionalism and gratitude.

7.1. Set Clear Goals

7.1.1. Define Objectives

- **Personal Goals:** Identify what you want to achieve during your internship, such as acquiring specific skills, gaining industry knowledge, or understanding particular job functions.
- **Professional Goals:** Consider how the internship can help you advance your career, such as building your resume, expanding your professional network, or exploring potential job opportunities.

7.1.2. Discuss Goals with Your Supervisor

- **Initial Meeting:** During your first week, have a conversation with your supervisor to discuss your goals and expectations.

- **Align Goals:** Ensure your goals align with the team's objectives and the tasks you'll be assigned.

7.2. Build Strong Relationships
7.2.1. Network with Colleagues

- **Introduce Yourself:** Take the initiative to introduce yourself to colleagues, team members, and other interns.
- **Attend Events:** Participate in team meetings, social events, and networking opportunities to connect with others.

7.2.2. Seek a Mentor

- **Find a Mentor:** Identify a mentor within the organization who can provide guidance, feedback, and career advice.
- **Regular Check-Ins:** Schedule regular meetings with your mentor to discuss your progress and seek advice.

7.3. Take Initiative
7.3.1. Volunteer for Projects

- **Proactive Approach:** Look for opportunities to contribute beyond your assigned tasks. Volunteer for additional projects or responsibilities that align with your interests and goals.
- **Show Enthusiasm:** Demonstrate eagerness to learn and take on new challenges.

7.3.2. Offer Solutions

- **Identify Problems:** Observe processes and identify areas where you can offer improvements or solutions.
- **Propose Ideas:** Share your ideas with your supervisor or team, showing that you're engaged and thinking critically about your work.

7.4. Develop and Enhance Skills
7.4.1. Focus on Skill Development

- **Technical Skills:** Work on developing any technical skills related to your field, such as software, tools, or methodologies.
- **Soft Skills:** Improve soft skills like communication, teamwork, problem-solving, and time management.

7.4.2. Seek Feedback

- **Request Feedback:** Regularly ask for constructive feedback from your supervisor and colleagues.
- **Act on Feedback:** Use the feedback to make improvements and enhance your performance.

7.5. Manage Your Time Effectively
7.5.1. Prioritize Tasks

- **Task Management:** Prioritize tasks based on their importance and deadlines. Use tools like to-do lists or project management software to stay organized.
- **Avoid Procrastination:** Stay on top of deadlines and complete tasks in a timely manner.

7.5.2. Balance Work and Learning

- **Workload Management:** Balance your workload to ensure you can handle your responsibilities without becoming overwhelmed.
- **Learning Opportunities:** Allocate time to learn about the company, industry, and any new skills or tools.

7.6. Reflect and Adapt
7.6.1. Regular Reflection

- **Evaluate Progress:** Periodically reflect on your progress and assess whether you're meeting your goals.
- **Adapt Goals:** Adjust your goals or strategies as needed based on your experiences and feedback.

7.6.2. Address Challenges

- **Identify Issues:** If you encounter challenges or difficulties, address them promptly by seeking advice or support.
- **Problem-Solving:** Approach challenges with a problem-solving mindset and be open to learning from setbacks.

7.7. Document Your Experience
7.7.1. Keep a Journal

- **Daily Log:** Maintain a journal to document your daily tasks, achievements, and reflections.
- **Learning Outcomes:** Note what you've learned from each experience or project.

7.7.2. Update Your Resume

- **Record Achievements:** Update your resume with the skills, experiences, and accomplishments gained during the internship.
- **Highlight Contributions:** Emphasize any significant projects or contributions you made.

7.8. Seek Feedback and Final Evaluation
7.8.1. Request a Final Review

- **Performance Review:** Request a final performance review from your supervisor to discuss your overall performance and receive feedback.
- **Discuss Strengths and Areas for Improvement:** Use the feedback to understand your strengths and identify areas for future development.

7.8.2. Express Gratitude

- **Thank You Notes:** Send thank you notes to your supervisor, team members, and anyone who has supported you during your internship.
- **Show Appreciation:** Express your gratitude for the opportunity and the support you received.

7.9. Leverage the Experience for Future Opportunities
7.9.1. Network for Future Connections

- **Stay in Touch:** Keep in contact with the people you met during your internship. Connect on LinkedIn and engage with them periodically.
- **Seek Recommendations:** Ask for recommendations or references from your supervisor and colleagues.

7.9.2. Explore Job Opportunities

- **Inquire About Full-Time Positions:** If you're interested in working with the company after your internship, inquire about potential full-time opportunities or openings.
- **Apply for Jobs:** Use the experience and connections from your internship to apply for future job positions.

7.10. Continuous Learning and Improvement
7.10.1. Evaluate Your Experience

- **Post-Internship Review:** Reflect on your overall internship experience, including what you enjoyed and what could be improved.
- **Learn from Experience:** Use the insights gained from your internship to guide your future career decisions and professional development.

7.10.2. Continue Professional Development

- **Skill Enhancement:** Continue to build on the skills and knowledge gained during your internship.
- **Industry Engagement:** Stay engaged with the industry through reading, networking, and attending relevant events.

CHAPTER EIGHT

Overcoming Challenges

Internships can be a valuable learning experience, but they also come with their own set of challenges. Overcoming these challenges effectively can enhance your internship experience and contribute to your professional growth. It is also important to deal with difficult situations and office politics. Balancing internship responsibilities with other commitments is very challenging. One common challenge in internships is adapting to a new work environment. The transition from academic settings to a professional workplace can be significant, with different expectations, cultures, and dynamics. To overcome this, approach the situation with an open mind and a willingness to learn. Observe the organizational culture and adapt to the new work norms. Actively seek feedback from your supervisor and colleagues to understand how you can align with the team's expectations. Demonstrating flexibility and a positive attitude can help ease this transition and integrate you more smoothly into the work environment. Another challenge often faced is managing multiple tasks and deadlines. Internships can involve a variety of responsibilities, and balancing these can sometimes be overwhelming. To manage this effectively, prioritize your tasks based on deadlines and importance. Use organizational tools such as to-do lists, calendars, or project management software to keep track of your responsibilities and deadlines. Communicate with your supervisor if you find yourself struggling to meet deadlines or if you need clarification on priorities. Effective time management and clear communication are key to handling multiple tasks successfully. Conflict or difficulties in working with colleagues can also pose challenges. Differences in work styles, communication preferences, or personality clashes can arise. To address these issues, practice active listening and strive to understand your colleagues' perspectives. Approach conflicts with a solution-oriented mindset and aim to resolve issues through constructive dialogue. Building strong interpersonal skills and demonstrating professionalism can help navigate these challenges and foster a more collaborative work environment. Another potential challenge is dealing with unclear or changing expectations. At times, the scope of your tasks might be ambiguous, or priorities may shift as projects evolve. To overcome this, seek clarity from your supervisor about your responsibilities and the expected outcomes. Regular check-ins and updates can help ensure you are aligned with the current goals and expectations. Being adaptable and open to feedback can help you adjust to changing requirements and continue contributing effectively. In some cases, you might encounter a lack of meaningful work or limited opportunities to showcase your skills. This can be disheartening, but it's important to remain proactive. If you find yourself with fewer responsibilities than anticipated, express your interest in taking on additional tasks or projects that align with your interests and goals. Show initiative by proposing ideas or solutions that could benefit the organization. Taking ownership of your experience and seeking out opportunities can help you gain more from your internship. Finally, personal challenges, such as balancing the internship with academic commitments or other responsibilities, can also arise. Managing these demands requires careful planning and organization. Create a schedule that allows you to allocate sufficient time for both your internship and other obligations. Communicate with your supervisor if you encounter conflicts or need adjustments to your schedule. Developing strong time management skills and maintaining a balanced approach can help you navigate these personal challenges effectively.

8.1. Adapting to a New Environment

8.1.1 Challenge: Adjusting to Workplace Culture

Solution: Take time to observe and understand the company's culture, including communication styles, dress code, and social norms. Be open and adaptable, and don't hesitate to ask questions if you're unsure about any aspect of the culture.

8.1.2 Challenge: Navigating Office Politics

Solution: Focus on maintaining professionalism and building positive relationships with colleagues. Avoid engaging in office gossip and stay focused on your work and learning objectives.

8.2. Managing Workload and Time

8.2.1 Challenge: Balancing Multiple Tasks

Solution: Prioritize tasks based on deadlines and importance. Use organizational tools like to-do lists or project management apps to keep track of your responsibilities. Communicate with your supervisor if you're feeling overwhelmed and need support.

8.2.2 Challenge: Meeting Deadlines

Solution: Break larger tasks into smaller, manageable steps and set intermediate deadlines for each step. Plan your work schedule to allocate sufficient time for each task and avoid last-minute rushes.

8.3. Communicating Effectively

8.3.1 Challenge: Understanding Expectations

Solution: Clarify your role and responsibilities with your supervisor. Ask for detailed instructions and feedback to ensure you understand what is expected of you.

8.3.2 Challenge: Seeking Help When Needed

Solution: Don't be afraid to ask for help if you encounter difficulties. Reach out to your supervisor or colleagues for guidance. Being proactive in seeking assistance demonstrates your commitment to learning and growth.

8.4. Dealing with Unclear or Insufficient Guidance

8.4.1 Challenge: Lack of Direction

Solution: Take initiative by setting up regular check-ins with your supervisor to discuss your progress and clarify any uncertainties. Document your understanding of tasks and seek confirmation to ensure you're on the right track.

8.4.2 Challenge: Receiving Minimal Feedback

Solution: Request constructive feedback on your performance and projects. Ask specific questions to understand areas where you can improve and seek advice on how to enhance your work.

8.5. Handling Difficult Interactions

8.5.1 Challenge: Conflicts with Colleagues

Solution: Address conflicts calmly and professionally. Seek to understand the other person's perspective and find common ground. If necessary, involve a supervisor or HR representative to mediate and resolve the issue.

8.5.2 Challenge: Dealing with Unclear or Excessive Criticism

Solution: Approach criticism with an open mind and use it as an opportunity for growth. Seek specific examples and suggestions for improvement. If criticism is excessive or unfounded, discuss your concerns with your supervisor to find a resolution.

8.6. Managing Work-Life Balance

8.6.1 Challenge: Overworking or Burnout

Solution: Set clear boundaries between work and personal time. Ensure you take breaks and maintain a healthy work-life balance. Communicate with your supervisor if you feel overburdened and need to adjust your workload.

8.6.2 Challenge: Juggling Multiple Commitments

Solution: Create a schedule that accommodates your internship along with other commitments such as academic work or personal responsibilities. Prioritize tasks and manage your time effectively to balance all aspects of your life.

8.7. Addressing Skill Gaps

8.7.1 Challenge: Lack of Required Skills

Solution: Identify any skill gaps and take proactive steps to address them. Utilize online resources, workshops, or seek guidance from colleagues to improve your skills. Be honest about your skill levels and express a willingness to learn.

8.7.2 Challenge: Rapid Learning Curve

Solution: Approach new tasks with a positive attitude and a willingness to learn. Break down complex tasks into smaller parts and seek guidance when needed. Use resources like training materials or online courses to accelerate your learning.

8.8. Coping with Uncertainty

8.8.1 Challenge: Unclear Future Opportunities

Solution: Discuss your career aspirations with your supervisor and seek advice on potential career paths. Express your interest in learning about different roles or departments within the company to explore future opportunities.

8.8.2 Challenge: Facing Rejection or Limited Feedback

Solution: Take rejections or limited feedback as learning experiences. Seek feedback on how you can improve and use it to refine your skills and approach. Stay positive and continue to seek out new opportunities.

8.9. Overcoming Lack of Motivation

8.9.1 Challenge: Feeling Disengaged or Unmotivated

Solution: Set personal goals for the internship and remind yourself of the benefits and learning opportunities it offers. Find aspects of the work that interest you and seek out projects or tasks that align with your passions.

8.9.2 Challenge: Boredom with Routine Tasks

Solution: Communicate with your supervisor about your interest in more challenging or varied tasks. Look for opportunities to take on new responsibilities or projects that can provide a fresh perspective and keep you engaged.

8.10. Seeking Support

8.10.1 Challenge: Feeling Isolated or Unsupported

Solution: Reach out to colleagues, mentors, or your supervisor for support and guidance. Engage in team activities and seek opportunities to build relationships with others in the organization.

8.10.2 Challenge: Navigating Organizational Structure

Solution: Take time to understand the organizational structure and identify key people who can provide support and guidance. Use this understanding to navigate the company effectively and seek help when needed.

8.11. Reflect and Learn

8.11.1 Challenge: Evaluating Your Experience

Solution: Regularly reflect on your experiences and progress. Consider what you've learned, what challenges you've overcome, and how you can apply these lessons to your future career.

8.11.2 Challenge: Identifying Growth Areas

Solution: After overcoming challenges, assess areas where you've grown and areas where you still need improvement. Set goals for continued development and seek additional opportunities to enhance your skills.

CHAPTER NINE

Post-Internship Opportunities

This is very important to evaluate the internship experience, Leveraging the internship for future job opportunities, and maintaining professional connections. One of the most promising opportunities is securing a full-time job offer from the same organization. Many companies use internships as a pipeline for future talent, evaluating interns as potential candidates for permanent roles. If you have demonstrated strong performance, fit well with the company culture, and shown a proactive attitude, you might be offered a position upon graduation. This seamless transition from intern to employee provides a solid foundation for your career and minimizes the job search process after completing your studies. Networking is another key aspect of post-internship opportunities. During your internship, you likely built valuable relationships with professionals, mentors, and peers. Maintaining these connections can be instrumental in finding future job opportunities. Reach out to your network for job leads, recommendations, or advice as you enter the job market. These professional contacts can provide valuable referrals, insights, and support in your job search.

Additionally, the skills and experiences gained during your internship can significantly enhance your employability. Use your internship experience to update your resume and highlight your achievements and acquired skills. A well-documented internship experience can make you a more competitive candidate in the job market. Be prepared to discuss your internship projects, accomplishments, and the value you added to the organization during interviews for future positions. Another opportunity is to leverage your internship experience for further educational pursuits. Your exposure to a specific field or industry might inspire you to pursue advanced studies or specialized certifications. Consider how the insights gained during your internship could influence your educational and career goals, and explore programs or courses that align with your new interests. Moreover, internships often provide a clearer understanding of your career goals and aspirations. Reflect on what you enjoyed and learned during your internship, and use this knowledge to refine your career path

9.1. Reflecting on Your Internship Experience

9.1.1. Self-Assessment

- **Evaluate Your Experience:** Reflect on your roles, responsibilities, and projects during the internship. Consider what you learned, the skills you developed, and how the experience aligns with your career goals.
- **Identify Strengths and Weaknesses:** Assess the skills you excelled in and areas where you encountered challenges. This will help you understand your growth and areas needing improvement.

9.1.2. Document Your Achievements

- **Update Your Resume:** Add new skills, experiences, and accomplishments to your resume. Highlight specific projects, contributions, and any measurable impacts you made.
- **Prepare a Portfolio:** If applicable, compile work samples, reports, or projects that showcase your contributions. A well-organized portfolio can be a powerful tool for job applications.

9.2. Networking and Relationship Building

9.2.1. Maintain Connections

- **Stay in Touch:** Regularly update and connect with colleagues, mentors, and supervisors from your internship. Share your achievements and career developments.
- **Engage on Social Media:** Use platforms like LinkedIn to maintain professional relationships. Engage with posts, share relevant content, and contribute to discussions.

9.2.2. Request Recommendations and References

- **Ask for Recommendations:** Request letters of recommendation from your supervisor or colleagues. Provide them with specific examples of your work to include in their recommendations.
- **Secure References:** Ensure that you have reliable references who can vouch for your skills and work ethic. Keep their contact information updated and maintain good relationships.

9.3. Exploring Job Opportunities

9.3.1. Full-Time Positions

- **Inquire About Opportunities:** If you enjoyed your internship, ask about potential full-time positions within the company. Express your interest in continuing to contribute to the organization.
- **Apply for Openings:** Look for job openings in companies where you interned. Tailor your applications to highlight your internship experience and how it prepares you for the role.

9.3.2. Industry Research

- **Explore Job Markets:** Research the job market for your industry to understand current trends, required skills, and potential employers.
- **Identify Key Employers:** Make a list of companies that align with your career interests and values. Look for job openings and networking opportunities within these organizations.

9.4. Continuing Education and Professional Development

9.4.1. Pursuing Further Education

- **Graduate Programs:** Consider whether further education, such as a master's degree or certification, could enhance your career prospects.
- **Specialized Training:** Look for workshops, courses, or certifications related to your field that can build on the skills gained during your internship.

9.4.2. Professional Development

- **Join Professional Associations:** Become a member of industry-related organizations to access resources, networking opportunities, and industry updates.
- **Attend Conferences and Workshops:** Participate in industry conferences, seminars, and workshops to stay updated on trends and expand your knowledge.

9.5. Leveraging Your Internship Experience

9.5.1. Highlighting Skills and Experience

- **Showcase Achievements:** In job applications and interviews, emphasize the skills and experiences gained during your internship. Provide concrete examples of your accomplishments.
- **Demonstrate Growth:** Use your internship experience to illustrate how you've grown professionally and how it has prepared you for future roles.

9.5.2. Articulating Your Value

- **Craft Your Narrative:** Develop a compelling narrative that connects your internship experience with your career goals. Be prepared to discuss how your experiences have shaped your professional aspirations.
- **Prepare for Interviews:** Practice articulating your internship experience and its relevance to the roles you are applying for. Be ready to discuss specific projects, challenges, and contributions

9.6. Exploring Alternative Career Paths

9.6.1. Considering Different Roles

- **Explore Related Fields:** If you discovered new interests or skills during your internship, explore related fields or roles that align with these interests.
- **Assess Transferable Skills:** Identify skills from your internship that are applicable to different roles or industries. Consider how these skills can be leveraged in alternative career paths.

9.6.2. Entrepreneurship and Freelancing

- **Explore Entrepreneurship:** If you have a passion or business idea, consider exploring entrepreneurship. Use your internship experience to develop a business plan or start a venture.
- **Freelancing Opportunities:** Explore freelancing opportunities if you prefer flexible work arrangements. Use your skills and experience to offer services on a freelance basis.

9.7. Evaluating Job Offers

9.7.1. Assessing Job Offers

- **Evaluate Compensation:** Consider the salary, benefits, and overall compensation package offered by potential employers. Ensure it meets your financial needs and career goals.
- **Review Company Culture:** Assess whether the company's culture, values, and work environment align with your preferences and career aspirations.

9.7.2. Negotiating Offers

- **Prepare for Negotiation:** Research typical salaries for the role and industry to support your negotiation. Be prepared to discuss your internship experience and its value.

- **Negotiate Terms:** Discuss salary, benefits, and other terms with potential employers. Be clear about your expectations and be open to compromise.

9.8. Transitioning to a Full-Time Role

9.8.1. Onboarding and Integration

- **Prepare for Onboarding:** Familiarize yourself with the company's onboarding process and requirements. Ensure you complete any necessary paperwork and training.
- **Integrate into the Team:** Build relationships with new colleagues and adapt to the company's culture. Be proactive in understanding your role and responsibilities.

9.8.2. Setting Goals

- **Establish Professional Goals:** Set clear, achievable goals for your first few months in the new role. Identify key objectives and milestones to guide your performance and development.
- **Seek Feedback:** Regularly seek feedback from your supervisor and colleagues to understand your performance and areas for improvement.

9.9. Building a Career Path

9.9.1. Career Planning

- **Develop a Career Plan:** Create a long-term career plan that outlines your goals, desired roles, and steps to achieve them. Use your internship experience to inform your career strategy.

- **Seek Career Guidance:** Consult with career advisors, mentors, or industry professionals to refine your career plan and explore potential opportunities.

9.9.2. Setting Milestones

- **Track Progress:** Regularly review your progress towards career goals and milestones. Adjust your plan as needed based on new opportunities or changes in your interests.
- **Celebrate Achievements:** Acknowledge and celebrate your achievements and progress. Recognize the milestones you've reached and use them as motivation for future goals.

9.10. Staying Engaged and Motivated

9.10.1. Continuous Learning

- **Pursue Learning Opportunities:** Stay engaged with ongoing learning and professional development. Seek out new skills and knowledge to enhance your career.
- **Stay Informed:** Keep up with industry trends, news, and developments to stay relevant and informed in your field.

9.10.2. Maintain Work-Life Balance

- **Balance Priorities:** Ensure you maintain a healthy work-life balance as you transition into a full-time role. Prioritize your well-being and personal life alongside your career goals.
- **Set Boundaries:** Establish boundaries between work and personal time to avoid burnout and maintain overall satisfaction.

9.11. Navigating Career Transitions

9.11.1. Handling Job Changes

- **Plan for Transitions:** If you decide to move on from a role, plan your transition carefully. Consider your next steps and how to communicate your departure professionally.
- **Seek New Opportunities:** Leverage your network and experiences to explore new job opportunities or career paths. Use your internship experience to guide your transition.

9.11.2. Managing Career Growth

- **Set Long-Term Goals:** Continuously set and review long-term career goals. Adjust your career plan based on your experiences and evolving aspirations.
- **Seek Advancement Opportunities:** Look for opportunities for advancement within your organization or industry. Pursue promotions, new roles, or additional responsibilities to further your career.

CHAPTER TEN

Internship Statistics

Obtaining an academic degree is just one aspect of career development. In fact, the latest internship statistics show that pursuing practical knowledge before employment gives job seekers a competitive edge on the labor market. Internship statistics offer valuable insights into the impact, trends, and effectiveness of internship programs across various industries and educational levels. Analyzing these statistics helps students, employers, and educational institutions understand the benefits of internships and identify areas for improvement. A significant statistic to consider is the employment outcomes associated with internships. Research consistently shows that internships are a strong predictor of future employment. For example, a study by the National Association of Colleges and Employers (NACE) found that 70% of interns receive job offers from the companies where they interned. This high conversion rate highlights the effectiveness of internships as a pipeline for full-time employment. Internships provide a platform for students and recent graduates to demonstrate their skills, fit with company culture, and potential for future roles, leading many employers to offer permanent positions to their successful interns. Another critical statistic relates to the benefits of internships for skill development. According to a survey by LinkedIn, 91% of internship employers agree that internships are an effective way to build a skilled workforce. Interns often gain hands-on experience, learn industry-specific skills, and develop professional competencies that are highly valued in the job market. This practical experience is crucial for bridging the gap between academic learning and real-world application, and it significantly enhances the employability of interns. Internship statistics also shed light on the demographics and distribution of internships. Data from the Bureau of Labor Statistics (BLS) indicates that internship participation varies by field, with certain industries such as technology, finance, and engineering offering a higher number of internships compared to others. Additionally, internships are more prevalent in larger organizations, where structured internship programs are more common. The distribution of internships can impact accessibility, with students from certain educational backgrounds or geographical locations potentially facing fewer opportunities. Another important statistic is related to compensation. A report from the National Association of Colleges and Employers (NACE) highlights that while the majority of internships are paid, there is still a significant proportion of unpaid internships. As of recent data, approximately 43% of internships are unpaid. This discrepancy can create barriers for students from lower-income backgrounds, limiting their ability to participate in valuable internship experiences. The trend toward paid internships is growing, as more companies recognize the importance of compensating interns fairly and the benefits of attracting a diverse pool of candidates. Internship statistics also reveal trends in internship duration and structure. The typical internship lasts between 8 to 12 weeks, aligning with summer break periods for students. However, there is an increasing trend towards offering year-round internships, allowing students to gain experience while managing academic responsibilities. Flexible and remote internship options are also on the rise, reflecting the changing nature of work and the need for adaptability in internship programs. The impact of internships on academic performance is another area of interest. Studies have shown that students who participate in internships often have higher academic performance and are more likely to graduate. The practical experience gained through internships can reinforce academic learning and provide context for theoretical knowledge, leading to improved academic outcomes and a more profound understanding of their field of study.

10.1 Impact of covid- 19: Following the COVID-19 pandemic, internship numbers plummeted. Many employers canceled their training programs. Those who didn't cancel shifted towards online attendance.

However; despite all the changes, the value of the professional learning experience remains relevant well into 2022.

- Before COVID-19, internship rates were between 50% and 60%. However, recent research indicates a much lower number of 21.5%. (NSCI Report, 2021)
- Despite the expansion of remote work, in-person positions are still relevant. 47.8% of respondents attended in-person internships, compared to 44.9% who attended online. (NSCI Report, 2021)
- The average length of an internship is four and a half months. (NSCI Report, 2021)

- Internships have a high satisfaction rate, with 36.4% of respondents reporting being extremely satisfied. (NSCI Report, 2021)
- 67.3% of non-interns said they wanted to pursue one but couldn't because of different obstacles. (NSCI Report, 2021)
- For 59.4%, not knowing how to find an internship was the main reason for not taking one. (NSCI Report, 2021)
- The average intern recruitment process lasts for eight and a half months. (NACE, 2021)
- Open applications are the most common way to source potential interns. (NACE, 2021)
- 60% spent most of their time doing analytical and project management tasks. (NACE, 2021)
- 67.9% of students attend internships to gain experience in a specific career they'd like to pursue. 24.8% take internships to explore different career options. (NSCI Report, 2021)
- During the pandemic, 64% of companies that canceled internships did not offer compensation. (CompareCamp, 2020)
- Companies expect to hire more interns by 22.6% in the following academic year. This is the highest increase in the last ten years. (NACE, 2022)
- Non-profit agencies connecting graduates with employers say they plan to hire 31.6% more interns than the previous year. (NACE, 2022)
- Typically, organizations begin their intern recruitment process approximately eight months in advance. (NACE, 2022)
- Most employers source students through open applications. (NACE, 2022)

- Even though 58.6% of the student population is female, about 43% of interns were women. (NACE, 2022)
- More than half of organizations plan to increase their college hires, and 41% plan to maintain it. (NACE, 2022)
- 66.1% of employers plan to hire graduates with a finance degree in the next year. 65% will employ accounting graduates, and 61.3% will look for candidates with a business administration or marketing degree. (NACE, 2022)
- 38% of employers run ongoing recruitment campaigns for interns throughout the year. (ISE, 2022)
- Between 21.5% to 50% of university students intern while in school. (CCWT, 2022)

10.2. Highest-paying Internship:
Tech, finance, and consulting are among the highest paying industries. Of course, there are exceptions to the rule. After a challenging few years that resulted in a shortage of opportunities, statistics show that the market's slowly recovering.

- The highest paying internship is with Roblox, with an average monthly income of $9,667. (Glassdoor, 2022)
- 71% of full-time interns received a salary, compared to just 26% of those who interned part-time. (NBER, 2020)
- 43% didn't receive compensation for their work. (CCWT, 2021)
- The job success rate for those with paid internships is 66.4%, compared to 43.7% for unpaid ones. (NACE, 2019)
- Other high-paying internships include leading tech companies like Amazon, Meta, Microsoft, Apple, and Google. (Glassdoor, 2022)

- Employers are more likely to respond to candidates applying for unpaid internships. (NBER, 2020)
- 62.4% of respondents were satisfied with their compensation. (CCWT, 2020)
- Only 14% of employers offer a signing bonus. (NACE, 2021)
- On average, a signing bonus is shy of $2,500. (CompareCamp, 2020)
- Between 500.000 and a million Americans work for no compensation. (CompareCamp, 2020)
- 26% of employers offer 401ks, while less than 18% offer medical insurance. (CompareCamp, 2020)
- Company culture is essential to the new generation workforce, as 88% prioritize meaning over money. (Tallo, 2021)
- The percentage of unpaid internships is between 30.8% to 58.1%. (CCWT, 2022)
- Among women, 54.3% took an unpaid internship, and 45.7% received compensation. On the other hand, 75.9% of men were compensated compared to 24.1% who didn't get paid. (CCWT, 2022)
- First-generation students were more likely to take unpaid internships (52%) than non-first-generation students (39%). (CCWT, 2022)

10.3. Internship Industry Statistics: The farming, fishing, and forestry industry have some of the lowest demands for internships. The highest demand is in business and financial operations, arts, design, media, and sales.

Check out more of the latest internship industry stats.

- Nine out of ten of the highest paying internships for 2022 are in the tech industry. (Glassdoor, 2022)

- Engineering internships pay an average salary of $61,380. (Glassdoor, 2022)
- Internships in STEM-related fields, social science, and health are more difficult to find than in other fields. (NSCI Report, 2021)
- More than half of interns in architecture and engineering, sales, and construction and extraction get paid. (NBER, 2020)
- Employees with high internship rates are law clerks (86%), audit associates (85%), reporters (82%), and analysts (77%). (CompareCamp, 2020)
- One-third of all insurance agents, real estate agents, and system administrators interned before getting a permanent job. (CompareCamp, 2020)
- Almost nine out of ten employees in Congress attend an internship. (CompareCamp, 2020)
- More than 60% of interns in the U.S. House of Representatives don't get a salary. (CompareCamp, 2020)

10.4. Internships & Job Success Statistics

In saturated job markets, internships give candidates an advantage. Employers appreciate a rich resume and candidates who already possess some of the necessary skills.

Internship consultants can further ease the process by connecting prospective candidates with their preferred employers. And although extra work in the field can't guarantee a job, it certainly helps.

10.5 Key Internship Statistics

- Irrespective of country, if it is possible, **74%** of interns receive a permanent job offer from the company

- Globally, companies save **$2 billion** dollar every year by offering internships
- Globally, around **500,000 to 10,00,000** internships are unpaid.
- On a global level, **51%** of the interns prefer it on-site.
- On average men tend to earn more, than women resulting in **$83,676 and $76,272** respectively.
- According to **NACE** unpaid internships are mostly completed by women
- Chegg Internships states that **65.7%** have their internships completed
- Furthermore, Chegg says, **2%** of the student population worldwide, do more than 6 internships in their educational period.
- Engineering internships can offer **$65,208** per annum on an average level.
- According to Glassdoor, NVIDIA a software company in the US offers the highest-ever scholarships to its interns resulting in **$8,811** as monthly pay.
- Interns are eligible to earn a bonus on their work quality of more than **$2,500**
- NACE provided the information that, globally **57.5%** of people received a full-time job offer after the internship
- The retention rate for up to 1 **year is 71.4%** with the same company
- **60%** of employers all over the world, always prefer those who have gained experience during the internship

CHAPTER ELEVEN

Internship – Key Points

11.1 Summary of Internship Impact

11.1.1. Personal and Professional Growth

Internships serve as a bridge between academic learning and professional experience. They offer students and early-career professionals the opportunity to apply theoretical knowledge in real-world settings, enhancing their skills and competencies. Key areas of growth include:

- **Skill Development:** Interns often acquire practical skills that are critical in their field of study. These skills include technical abilities, problem-solving techniques, and project management capabilities.
- **Career Exploration:** Internships allow individuals to explore different career paths, understand industry demands, and identify their professional interests and strengths.
- **Professional Networking:** Interns build valuable connections with professionals, mentors, and peers, which can lead to future job opportunities and collaborations.

11.1.2. Organizational Benefits

For organizations, internships offer several advantages, including:

- **Talent Pipeline:** Internships provide a pool of potential future employees who are already familiar with the company's culture and operations.
- **Fresh Perspectives:** Interns bring new ideas and perspectives that can drive innovation and improvements within the organization.
- **Increased Productivity:** Interns often contribute to ongoing projects and help alleviate workloads, enhancing overall productivity.

11.2. Key Learnings from Internships

11.2.1. Impact on Interns

- **Real-World Experience:** Interns gain hands-on experience that complements their academic learning, making them more competitive in the job market.
- **Soft Skills Development:** Internships foster the development of essential soft skills, such as communication, teamwork, and time management.
- **Career Clarity:** Internships help individuals gain clarity about their career goals and professional interests, guiding their future career choices.

11.2.2. Impact on Organizations

- **Skill Enhancement:** Organizations benefit from the diverse skills and fresh perspectives that interns bring, which can lead to innovative solutions and improvements.
- **Talent Acquisition:** Successful internships often lead to full-time employment offers, helping organizations retain top talent.
- **Brand Ambassadorship:** Interns who have positive experiences become advocates for the company, enhancing its reputation as a desirable employer.

11.3. Best Practices for Successful Internships

11.3.1. For Interns

- **Proactive Engagement:** Interns should actively seek learning opportunities, take initiative, and be open to feedback to maximize their internship experience.
- **Professionalism:** Maintaining a high level of professionalism, including punctuality, dress code, and communication, is crucial for a successful internship.
- **Goal Setting:** Setting clear goals and objectives for the internship helps in tracking progress and achieving desired outcomes.

11.3.2. For Organizations

- **Structured Programs:** Designing a structured internship program with clear objectives, training, and mentorship ensures a productive experience for both the intern and the organization.
- **Effective Onboarding:** A comprehensive onboarding process helps interns integrate smoothly into the

organization and understand their roles and responsibilities.

- **Feedback Mechanisms:** Regular feedback and performance reviews provide interns with constructive insights and help in their professional development.

11.4. Challenges and Solutions

11.4.1. Common Challenges

- **Unclear Expectations:** Interns may face challenges due to unclear roles or expectations, which can impact their performance and experience.
- **Limited Learning Opportunities:** Internships that involve mostly administrative tasks can limit the learning and growth opportunities for interns.
- **Integration Issues:** Interns may struggle to integrate into the team or company culture, affecting their overall experience.

11.4.2. Addressing Challenges

- **Clear Communication:** Setting clear expectations and providing detailed job descriptions can help interns understand their roles and responsibilities.
- **Diverse Experiences:** Offering a variety of tasks and projects ensures that interns gain comprehensive experience and exposure to different aspects of the organization.
- **Support Systems:** Providing mentorship and support helps interns navigate integration challenges and feel valued within the organization.

11.5. The Future of Internships

11.5.1. Evolving Trends

- **Remote Internships:** The rise of remote work has led to the growth of virtual internships, offering flexibility and broader access to opportunities.
- **Increased Focus on Diversity:** Organizations are placing greater emphasis on diversity and inclusion in their internship programs to attract a wider range of talent.
- **Integration of Technology:** The use of technology and digital tools is enhancing the internship experience, from virtual onboarding to project management.

11.5.2. Future Recommendations

- **Enhanced Collaboration:** Encouraging collaboration between educational institutions and organizations can improve the quality and effectiveness of internship programs.
- **Continuous Improvement:** Regularly assessing and updating internship programs based on feedback from interns and employers ensures ongoing relevance and success.

Conclusion

In conclusion, internships play a pivotal role in shaping careers and driving organizational progress. Their continued evolution and adaptation will ensure that they remain a vital component of professional development and career readiness.

Navigating the professional landscape as an intern can often feel like starting at the bottom of the career hierarchy. However, it's crucial to understand and embrace your intrinsic value within the organization. Even if your contributions seem small or behind-the-scenes, they play a significant role in the broader organizational context and are genuinely valued

Internships, while they may present their own set of challenges, offer an unparalleled opportunity for growth. While challenges are a natural part of any new role, they also contribute to your learning and development. By recognizing the value of your contributions and remaining open to growth, you can make the most of your internship experience and set a solid foundation for your future career.

Remember that internships are valuable experiences that can shape your career path. Stay motivated, keep learning, and embrace every opportunity that comes your way!

Future belongs to those who burn, learn and earn.

"Burn" – Passion and Dedication

To excel in an internship, it's essential to bring a high level of passion and commitment. **"Burn"** represents the enthusiasm and drive you need to tackle challenges and go beyond basic expectations. Showcasing your dedication through hard work and proactive involvement can set you apart and leave a lasting impression on your supervisors.

"Learn" – Continuous Growth

Internships are prime opportunities for learning and personal development. **"Learn"** signifies the importance of absorbing new skills, gaining insights, and adapting to the workplace environment. Embrace every learning opportunity, seek feedback, and be open to new experiences. This proactive approach to learning can significantly enhance your skills and broaden your professional knowledge.

"Earn" – Achievements and Rewards

In an internship, **"earn"** reflects the tangible and intangible rewards you gain from your experience. This could include valuable skills, professional connections, or even potential job offers. It also emphasizes the importance of earning respect and recognition through your contributions and efforts. Ultimately, the growth and achievements you gain from the internship can pave the way for future career opportunities.

By embodying the principles of burning passion, continuous learning, and earning rewards, you can maximize the value of your internship experience. These elements collectively help you build a strong foundation for your future career, positioning you as a motivated and capable candidate in the professional world.

www.ingramcontent.com/pod-product-compliance
Lightning Source LLC
Chambersburg PA
CBHW021546150726
47990CB00006B/2418